Studies in Natural Language Processing

Memory and context for language interpretation

Studies in Natural Language Processing

Executive Editor: Aravind K. Joshi
Sponsored by the Association for Computational Linguistics

This series publishes monographs, texts, and edited volumes within the interdisciplinary field of computational linguistics. Sponsored by the Association for Computational Linguistics, the series represents the range of topics of concern to the scholars working in this increasingly important field, whether their background is in formal linguistics, psycholinguistics, cognitive psychology or artificial intelligence.

Also in this series:
Natural language parsing, edited by David R. Dowty, Lauri Karttunen and Arnold Zwicky
Text generation by Kathleen R. McKeown
Language and spatial cognition Annette Herskovits
Computational linguistics by Ralph Grishman
Semantic interpretation and the resolution of ambiguity by Graeme Hirst
Machine translation, edited by Sergei Nirenburg

Memory and context for language interpretation

HIYAN ALSHAWI
SRI International Cambridge
Computer Science Research Centre

CAMBRIDGE UNIVERSITY PRESS

CAMBRIDGE

LONDON NEW YORK NEW ROCHELLE

MELBOURNE SYDNEY

CAMBRIDGE UNIVERSITY PRESS
Cambridge, New York, Melbourne, Madrid, Cape Town, Singapore, São Paulo, Delhi

Cambridge University Press
The Edinburgh Building, Cambridge CB2 8RU, UK

Published in the United States of America by Cambridge University Press, New York

www.cambridge.org
Information on this title: www.cambridge.org/9780521103589

First published 1987
This digitally printed version 2009

A catalogue record for this publication is available from the British Library

ISBN 978-0-521-34059-5 hardback
ISBN 978-0-521-10358-9 paperback

Contents

Part II

Preface

The open ended nature of the influence of extra-sentential context on natural language interpretation has impeded developments in computer language processing. Several problems in the field, including reference resolution, word sense disambiguation, and compound noun interpretation, require mechanisms for exploiting the discourse context and knowledge of the discourse domain. The research reported in this book is an attempt to provide such mechanisms for a relatively unified treatment of language processing problems which are usually studied in isolation. The proposed mechanisms were designed with a view to simplicity and efficiency and do not provide advanced capabilities for reasoning about the plausibility of interpretations or about the intentions of discourse participants. These restrictions result in a computationally effective approach to handling the more common and straightforward cases of ambiguity and reference that arise during language interpretation. The mechanisms depend on simple relationships between entities in the discourse domain, and on the relative salience of these entities imposed by the discourse context. Computational tractability is maintained by relying heavily on marker processing, a very restricted processing model.

The material in the book is a reorganized version of the material presented in my doctoral thesis (entitled *Memory and Context Mechanisms for Automatic Text Processing*) which was completed in December 1983. In the original thesis there was less of a separation between the proposed mechanisms, discussed in Part I of the book, and their embodiment in an experimental text processing system described in Part II.

I am glad to have this opportunity to thank those who made it possible for me to work on this subject for three years as my thesis topic, and on other topics in computational linguistics for another two years at the University of Cambridge Computer Laboratory. In particular, I am grateful to Karen Sparck Jones for her enthusiastic, though liberal, approach to supervising doctoral research; Roger Needham for the pleasant and productive atmosphere at the Laboratory; Bran Boguraev for making his parsing system available; and Antonia Lovelace, and my parents Khalid and Dorothy, for their generous support and encouragement. The Committee of Vice-chancellors and Principals, Trinity Hall, and the Science and Engineering Research Council provided funds during this period.

Part I

1

Introduction

1.1. Language interpretation problems

Before we can claim to have a reasonable understanding of natural language processing, we need reasonable models of semantic and pragmatic interpretation. While others have worked towards this goal within the artificial intelligence paradigm much of their work has focused on solving particular interpretation problems, such as the resolution of definite references (e.g. Sidner 1979) and the understanding of compound nouns (e.g. McDonald 1982). This book, instead of making an in-depth study of a particular problem in language interpretation, presents a relatively unified framework for solving a class of (English) interpretation problems.

This class includes many cases of reference resolution, word sense disambiguation, and the interpretation of implicit relationships. These problems are important in the sense that they are pervasive; solving them is necessary for the successful interpretation of almost any English discourse. Countless examples exhibiting these problems are discussed in the literature, for example in the references cited below. I have chosen to use the neutral term "language interpretation problem" because the language processing issues with which we will be concerned cover phenomena which span both semantic and pragmatic interpretation processes; they require exploiting lexical semantics, knowledge of the discourse domain, and the influence of context.

The types of interpretation problem which can be handled by our framework are basically those which can be solved by using certain simple relationships between objects present in memory (roughly, certain types of meaning postulate in the case of word senses), and those which can be formulated in terms of choosing between such objects on the basis of the current discourse context. (For the moment we can take memory to be any repository of information relevant to the language interpretation process.) It is not surprising, therefore, that the central mechanisms provided by this framework for language interpretation are a memory mechanism and a context mechanism. I will describe these mechanisms in Chapter 2.

Excluded from the cases of language interpretation problems which these mechanisms are intended to solve are those which involve complex reasoning, such as reasoning by cases or with incomplete knowledge, or reasoning about the intentions of discourse participants. Nor do they include fine judgment of the plausibility of the alternative interpretations suggested by an understanding process. Instead, the solution of interpretation problems by our framework will depend on more or less direct application of linguistic and world knowledge represented in memory, and of the contextual information managed by the context mechanism. This restriction is motivated by an attempt to maximize the "performance/complexity" ratio of the mechanisms provided by a framework for solving the most common and simple language interpretation problems. The approach can thus also be regarded as an investigation into the extent to which we can carry out language interpretation without powerful reasoning mechanisms.

Because the computational framework adopted for the interpretation mechanisms has the flavor of a marker propagation or spreading activation model, I will refer to it as "marker processing". This kind of model was chosen not only because it is a simple computational framework but because it provides interpretation mechanisms which are efficient or at least computationally tractable. Some artificial intelligence researchers interested in the efficient use of knowledge in intelligent systems have proposed hardware designs for implementing marker propagation. Fahlman's NETL (Fahlman 1980) and the Connection Machine (Hillis 1981) allow a very high degree of parallelism when performing marker propagations for memory retrieval. The work reported here is therefore relevant to evaluating the feasibility of applying such hardware designs to natural language processing. An alternative way of taking advantage of the simplicity of marker processing was developed in the form of software techniques, for conventional hardware, which allow more efficient implementation of the language interpretation mechanisms in terms of marker processing (Chapter 8).

Marker processing, seen as "spreading activation", has also been proposed as a model of contextual influence on language interpretation (see e.g. Charniak 1983). As well as providing Fahlman-like memory retrieval, marker processing supports the context mechanism in our language interpretation framework too. However, the context mechanism employs marker processing in a more controlled way than the term spreading activation might suggest, allowing information provided by more structured models of discourse processing (see e.g. Grosz 1977) to be handled by the context mechanism.

Context based disambiguation with this mechanism depends on the derivation of "context activation" values from "context factors" (introduced in Chapter 2) which indicate contributions to foregrounding. Proposals for detailed mechanisms playing a similar role are rare in the linguistics literature. A notable exception is Kantor's notion of "degree of activatedness" (Kantor 1977) which he applied to the analysis of pronominal reference; but even Kantor's theory is not in a form that can be used as the basis for a computational model. Methods for choosing between remaining candidate referents after all linguistic constraints have been applied are usually not provided at all in formal linguistic research. An example of this is the work by Kamp which has nevertheless made significant advances in understanding such constraints in terms of building discourse representation structures (see Kamp's explicit remarks to this effect in Kamp 1981).

The goals of handling common interpretation problems, and of simplicity and efficiency, can be put forward as the motivation for our framework both in the context of modeling human language processing and of developing computer systems capable of performing natural language processing applications. However, the work reported in this book was really carried out in terms of the latter, i.e. automatic language processing, and I will avoid claims and suggestions about human language processing. Though studies of human language processing did influence this work as inputs to the design of our language interpretation framework, there was no attempt to justify the framework in such terms.

As I said above, the common language interpretation problems have been studied by researchers in artificial intelligence, and in our framework they are formulated in terms of searching for "memory entities" satisfying constraints and/or choosing between them according to the current context. Thus reference resolution involves searching for entities satisfying constraints derived from the text (cf. Mellish 1980) and choosing between them (cf. Sidner 1979). Similarly, word sense disambiguation can be seen as a process of applying semantic category restrictions (cf. Boguraev 1979) followed by context based disambiguation (cf. Hirst and Charniak 1982). Discovering implicit relationships implied by compound nouns, possessive constructions, and words such as "have" and "of" (cf. Grosz et al. 1982) depends on sentence based constraints as well as the application of contextual information for choosing between alternative candidate interpretations (cf. Steinacker and Trost 1983).

1.2. Memory, context, and focus

Given that there are no standard definitions, at present, for the terms "memory", "context", and "focus", some preliminary remarks about their use in this work and the relationships between them are in order. "Memory" has been used in artificial intelligence work on natural language processing to refer to the component which stores knowledge about the domain of discourse, about objects and predicates corresponding to word senses, and also perhaps the "results", whatever form these may take, of understanding the language input to a system (e.g. Rieger 1975; Small 1980; and Lebowitz 1983). However, the knowledge base components of other such systems (e.g. Walker 1978; Mark 1981; and Norton 1983) play a similar role, and for this reason the description "knowledge base component" could have been used in the description of this work instead of "memory mechanism". My use of the term "memory" does not imply any claims about modeling human use of knowledge for text understanding, and there is no attempt to limit the contents of memory solely to information of a linguistic or "real world" nature.

Much of the information made available by memory for supporting text processing is implicit, in the sense that it is not present explicitly as stand-alone statements. This is largely a consequence of the hierarchical nature of the memory representation: information is inherited from generic to more specific entities in memory. The extraction of this information, using the marker processing model mentioned already, will be referred to as "memory retrieval". One way of characterizing the role of "context" in our framework is that it constrains the searching involved in the memory retrieval process, and selects between the results of this process.

A broader definition of the context with respect to which a text is interpreted would have to include the whole of the contents of memory rather than just the information restricting retrieval from it. For the sake of having a clear distinction between memory and context, and in order to reduce the vagueness of the term, "context" will be used here to refer only to the relevance and salience information which restricts memory retrieval.

Still, this more restricted notion of context is not far off from the various artificial intelligence treatments of contextual influence. Thus a number of systems have approached the restriction problem by organizing the knowledge base into sections, or "frames", so that when one of these sections is activated, retrieval and inference are confined to the knowledge represented in that section (e.g. Charniak 1978). This approach is taken further when the activated structure (commonly called a "script") guides the interpretation of the text, interpretation becoming a process instantiating predictions made by the structure (e.g. DeJong 1979). Problems associated with such approaches include the difficulty of selecting an appropriate frame or script, and the over-rigid predictions which they make, especially those based on scripts.

Instead of restricting the retrieval process to information in a frame corresponding to the current context, Fahlman (1979) has advocated the use of parallel hardware as an alternative solution to the problem of enabling efficient deductive memory retrieval from a large knowledge base; the whole knowledge base is operated on in a well specified manner using marker processing (see Charniak 1982 for discussion). This parallel approach shifts the main use of context from constraining the scope of the input of retrieval operations towards choosing between alternatives, since the results of retrieval are now less likely to be unique.

The use of context to disambiguate between alternative results of memory retrieval is closely related to the notion of a current "focus". In our language interpretation framework, while context represents information about the salience of knowledge, focus specifies the entity, or group of entities, which are currently *most* salient. In other words, we will view focus as a derived notion determined by the available contextual information. Just as with context, keeping track of focus has efficiency implications since memory retrieval searches can begin with the items which are in focus (see Grosz 1977).

The model of context developed in this work is not just concerned with context application for restricting memory retrieval when solving interpretation problems. It also provides a computational mechanism for gradually accumulating, and combining, the influence of different kinds of information contributing to context (such as recency of mention, subject area, and syntactic marking of focus) as the processing of a text progresses.

1.3. The experimental text processing system

The mechanisms which I will propose in Part I for solving common interpretation problems also support the execution of a non-linguistic application task in an experimental text processing system embodying the mechanisms. The organizational structure and implementation of this program, called Capture, are described in Part II. It was designed to process collections of English paragraphs, for example museum records, and produces output which allows the incorporation of information derived from the texts into an existing conventional database. This database creation task does have potential practical applications, but it was chosen mainly because it requires solving language interpretation problems which occur in running text. Since explicit statements, intended for an external system, are produced, it is relatively easy, compared to tasks such as summarizing, to see whether or not the interpretation process has been successful. Appendix A contains several example texts processed by the Capture system, together with the "database creation statements" extracted from them.

Apart from its main role as a vehicle for testing language interpretation mechanisms, the Capture system also demonstrates an approach to representing and using the relationships between linguistic and non-linguistic knowledge in order to carry out a text processing application. The main challenge here was to design the system so that the language processing mechanisms were independent of discourse domain and application task; handling input to different databases should require only the addition of declarative memory assertions and new word sense entries in the lexicon. The design of the Capture system achieves this aim, qualified, of course, by the reality that new domains of discourse can introduce (general) language interpretation problems which may not have arisen in the treatment of previous domains.

Part II thus presents the Capture system as a detailed model, in the sense used in the artificial intelligence paradigm, of a text processing system embodying the language interpretation mechanisms discussed in Part I. As well as providing a weak sort of verification of the consistency of the framework based on the interpretation mechanisms, it also fleshes out, in one particular way, some of the possibilities admitted by this framework. Occasionally, for the sake of concreteness, I have described some of the more specific choices taken in the design of the Capture system in Part I, but these choices will be indicated explicitly, and I have presented any discussion of example paragraphs processed by the Capture system and the non-linguistic processing carried out by it exclusively in Part II. This should make it easier for the reader to distinguish the essentials of the proposed framework for language interpretation from idiosyncrasies of the experimental implementation.

In Part I the presentation of the language interpretation mechanisms begins with a description of the representation for memory and context, and the marker processing model, in Chapter 2. Chapter 3 proposes solutions, based on these mechanisms, to three basic interpretation problems mentioned earlier - reference resolution, word sense disambiguation, and relationship interpretation. Chapter 4 discusses the mechanisms and compares them with related artificial intelligence approaches. In Part II, Chapter 5 introduces the database capture application and gives an overview of the components and capabilities of the Capture system. Chapter 6 shows how the techniques developed in Part I are realized in the Capture system and applied to specific texts processed by it. Details of the implementation of the database capture component are considered in Chapter 7. This chapter goes into some of the more mundane aspects, necessary for a working system, of the whole process of sentence interpretation and database creation. Chapter 8 describes and evaluates the software techniques for enhancing the efficiency of the marker processing model on conventional machines. From the perspective of computational linguistics as a whole, this final chapter addresses rather specialized computational issues of our framework for memory and context processing, and so some readers may wish to regard it as a kind of appendix.

2
The mechanisms

As suggested in the introduction, the memory mechanism provides a minimal representation formalism for encoding relationships between word senses and other semantic "entities" while the context mechanism encodes information about the factors contributing to the salience of these entities in the current context. We now need to explain how these two types of information are represented by the mechanisms, and how the marker processing model provides the computational basis for processing this information so that it can be applied to the language interpretation problems discussed in Chapter 3.

2.1. Representation in memory

Entities and basic assertions

The memory contains *entities*, or concepts, which include generic and individual objects, predicates and relationships. However, entities are not categorized as belonging to one of these types, but instead, the type of an entity, and the way in which it takes part in memory processing, depends on how it is related to other entities in memory, and in particular on the organizational relationships which are being used to access it.

There are two kinds of basic assertions which give rise to these organizational relationships, *specializations* and *correspondences*. Specialization assertions have the form

(Specialization: A of B)

where A and B are memory entities. For example one specialization assertion is

(Specialization: computer of machine).

'Computer' can now be viewed as a "specialization" of 'machine', and also 'machine' as a "generalization" of 'computer'; i.e. things which can be described as computers can also be described as machines. (Single quotes denote memory entities. This convention applies throughout the text.) Assertions of this type form the specialization, or "is-a", hierarchy of entities in memory. Subtypes of the specialization assertion are used in order to distinguish whether generics or individuals are being related, as described later. The hierarchy is "tangled" (i.e. a partial order) in that an entity can be the specialization of more than one generic entity. Thus we could have

(Specialization: woman of human), and
(Specialization: woman of female).

There is a most generic entity 'thing' which has no generalizations. (The term "generic" will be used loosely to contrast entities with entities "lower" in the specialization hierarchy or correspondence hierarchy (see below) and also to indicate type-token distinctions.)

A correspondence assertion has the form

(Corresponds: C1 to D1 as C2 to D2),

where C1, D1, C2, and D2 are entities in memory. C1 is viewed as a "role", "argument", or "slot" of "owner" D1; and as a "role specialization" of C2, where C2 is viewed as a (generic) argument of D2. The pairs (C1, D1) and (C2, D2) are *role-owner* pairs. Examples of correspondence assertions are

(Corresponds: data/processing to computer as
machine/activity to machine)
(Corresponds: supplies/agent to supply as agent to verb/statement).

The correspondence assertions in memory form a hierarchy of ordered role-owner pairs, the most generic of which is ('role', 'thing'). This hierarchy complements the specialization hierarchy: while the specialization hierarchy forms a classification of the kinds of entities in memory, the correspondence hierarchy forms a classification of the relationships between them. A correspondence assertion states that there is a relationship between one (role-owner) pair of entities which is a refinement of a relationship which exists between another pair of entities in memory. The correspondence assertion allows the definition of arguments for concepts, i.e. what are called "roles" or "slots" in several representation formalisms. A correspondence assertion can thus be thought of as a role specialization assertion.

Normally, in these other formalisms, role specialization is taken to be an assertion between an owner, a generic role and a specialized role; and the equivalent to the first correspondence assertion can be paraphrased as "data/processing fills the machine/activity role for computer". However, this approach often leads to what is, perhaps, an artificial distinction and asymmetry between "concepts" and "roles" (this point is discussed further in Section 4.1). In contrast, any memory entity can take part as either "role" or "owner" in many correspondence assertions, but this does not lead to confusion because the fourth argument of the assertion, the "generic-owner", is present.

This description of the specialization and correspondence assertions, given mainly in terms of examples, is not intended to be a full characterization of the meaning of these assertion types. When viewed as part of the text processing system, the assertion types can be said to take their "meaning" from the operations which are used to process them, for example from the way in which specialization assertions take part in the resolution of referents for definite noun phrases such as "the machine", and from the way that correspondence assertions take part in the interpretation of compound nouns such as "computer processing". A description of how memory is used in a text processing system, such as the description of Capture in Part II, thus constitutes an informal operational semantics for the memory formalism. The coherence of such an operational semantics for the memory system depends, in the end, on how well the text processing system works. I would like to proceed by discussing another way of providing a semantics for memory assertions.

Semantics of memory assertions

As just indicated, we can think of structures in memory as gaining their meaning from the operations which make use of them in the text processing system. Another sort of semantics relates symbols to referents in the world (or possible worlds) which they describe, in a rigorous and formally satisfactory way. Some advantages of having such a semantics for representation systems are discussed by Patrick Hayes (1977a). There has also been a recent show of interest in providing denotational semantics for frame-like representations (see Reimer 1983 and Hahn for example). Hayes argues that the contribution of logic, as a representation system, is its model-theoretic semantic theory. In this type of semantics for logic conjoining predicate logic assertions restricts the set of possible interpretations for the symbols occurring in them. In an analogous way, we would like the addition of new memory assertions to restrict the interpretation of memory entities. ("Interpretation" is used here in a different sense from that given to it in other chapters where I have used it to refer to language interpretation.)

If we could indicate how a simple extensional semantics could be devised for the symbols and structures used in the memory representation formalism, this could then be used to validate memory operations, or to characterize other operations as approximate (i.e. not necessarily valid for all possible interpretations of the contents of memory). An interpretation is taken here to consist of functions which model the relationship between memory entities and entities in a particular world described by memory.

Given the set M of memory entities and a set W whose members are the objects in some (real or imaginary) world or domain of discourse, memory assertions stipulate restrictions on two interpretation functions, *ref* and *rel*. *Ref* maps a memory entity to the set of objects in the world to which the memory entity refers, i.e. the set of world entities which the memory entity may describe. *Rel* maps a role-owner pair of memory entities to the set of pairs of objects in the world, i.e. to a relation, which the pair in memory can describe. The ranges of the function *ref* and the partial function *rel* are as follows (where P stands for power set):

$$\text{ref} : \text{M} \rightarrow P(\text{W})$$

$$\text{rel} : \text{M} \times \text{M} \rightarrow P(\text{W}) \times P(\text{W}).$$

The basic constraints for a valid interpretation are as follows

(1) For any specialization assertion (Specialization: A of B) it must be true that

$$\text{ref(A)} \subseteq \text{ref(B)}.$$

(2) For any correspondence assertion (Corresponds: C1 to D1 as C2 to D2) these two constraints must hold

$$\text{rel(C1, D1)} \subseteq \text{rel(C2, D2)}$$

$$\text{rel(C1,D1)} \subseteq \text{ref(D1)} \times \text{ref(C1)}.$$

There are subtypes of the specialization and correspondence assertions, and these have further constraints associated with them which I will indicate shortly. One such constraint which can be shown to be relevant to the inheritance of properties is that *rel* must (in cases specified by the subtyping) yield a function when applied to certain role-owner pairs.

On the basis of these constraints it is possible to make a number of deductions which are consistent with a valid interpretation and which can be assumed to hold by the memory processing operations. We are here taking a deduction to be the derivation of a new memory assertion from a set of previous memory assertions in such a way that the conditions imposed by the new assertion are consistent with valid interpretations of the original assertions. These deductions include the transitivity of specialization and the inheritance of properties, as used by similar representation systems.

For example if we have the assertions

(Specialization: computer of machine), and
(Specialization: machine of inanimate)

then the validity of the interpretation will not change if

(Specialization: computer of inanimate)

is added to memory. The transitivity of correspondence assertions can also be justified, because it preserves (2) above. Thus from the following memory assertions

(Corresponds: manufacture/object to manufacture as
make1/object to make1)
(Corresponds: make1/object to make1 as object to verb/statement)

we can deduce that

(Corresponds: manufacture/object to manufacture as
object to verb/statement).

The processing model which I have adopted does not perform deductions in the manner described above explicitly, but instead performs memory retrieval operations whose results are sets of memory entities (see Section 2.3 below for an explanation of this processing model). Such an operation can be thought of as being based on "valid" inferences if the results of evaluating the operation do not vary when any deduced assertions (in the sense explained above) are included in memory. If an operation is not of this type, then it might be violating the conditions on valid interpretations imposed by the semantics of assertions and hence could be thought of as being an "approximate" operation. (The implemented Capture system does use such "approximate" operations when performing certain memory operations.) The formal semantic constraints are useful because we can, in principle, employ them to define a clear distinction between valid and approximate operations, and as a tool for determining whether individual operations are valid or only approximate.

Subtypes of assertions

The specialization and correspondence assertions can carry further information about the relationships between their arguments, encoded in the form of a list of flags given as an additional argument to the assertions. These flags and the additional semantic conditions associated with them are given below. In general, the subtypes provide a refinement of the basic structure imposed on memory by the two main assertion types.

If a specialization assertion is marked by the flag "instance", then the specialized entity can refer to only one world entity in an interpretation. Thus the assertion

(Specialization: A of B (instance))

imposes the additional condition

$|\mathrm{ref}(A)| = 1.$

(The notion of being an individual is taken, for the purpose of this work, to be a comment on how memory, and the language being processed, view and describe a real or imaginary world rather than some more fundamental comment about that which exists in that world.)

The flag "member" is stronger than "instance" and is used to make an explicit specification of all the individual entities described by a generic entity. The additional conditions for a (maximal) set of specialization assertions of the form

(Specialization: A_1 of B (member))...(Specialization: A_n of B (member))

are as follows ($1 \leqq i,j \leqq n$)

$|\mathrm{ref}(A_i)| = 1$
$\bigcup_{i=1,n} \mathrm{ref}(A_i) = \mathrm{ref}(B)$
$\mathrm{ref}(A_i) \neq \mathrm{ref}(A_j)$ if $i \neq j$.

The flag "distinct" can be attached to specialization assertions to indicate exclusive subcategorization of the entity being specialized. If for any entity B, there is a set of assertions of the form

(Specialization: A_1 of B (distinct))...(Specialization: A_n of B (distinct))

then the following is true ($1 \leqq i,j \leqq n$):

$ref(A_i) \cap ref(A_j) = \varnothing$ if $i \neq j$.

The import of the flags which can be associated with correspondence assertions is now explained in terms of *rel*.

(Corresponds: C1 to D1 as C2 to D2 (uni))

means that

rel(C1,D1) : ref(D1) $\rightarrow$ ref(C1)

is a function (total and single valued).

(Corresponds: C1 to D1 as C2 to D2 (rev))

means that

rel(C1,D1) : ref(D1) $\rightarrow$ ref(C1)

is a bijection (one-one and onto).

Examples of these assertions are

(Corresponds: mother to mothers/child as parent to child (uni)), and

(Corresponds: root to tree as node to directed/graph (rev)).

Thus the first assertion says that children have unique mothers, and the second one says that there is a one-to-one mapping between roots and trees viewed as directed graphs. The semantics guarantee that *uni* is inherited through correspondence assertions.

Since the constraints imposed by flags are cumulative, combinations of other more primitive flags are possible instead of some of those we have just defined for the memory formalism. For example, we can define a flag *cover* so that a (maximal) set of assertions of the form

(Specialization: A1 of B (cover)) ... (Specialization: An of B (cover))

implies that

$\cup_{i=1,n}$ ref(Ai) = ref(B).

In this case *member* would be redundant since it would be equivalent to the flag combination *(distinct instance cover)*. The flag *rev* can also be decomposed in terms of flags stating that the relationship satisfies *uni* and is "one-one" and "onto". The motivation for the choice of flags that were defined for the memory formalism is simply that these seem to be useful, in practice, for stating information at the level of detail expected of this kind of formalism.

The approach to co-reference of memory entities which I have taken in this framework is very simple. The semantics of the specialization assertion allows co-reference to be represented as mutual specialization, and the following assertions state that the memory entities A and B co-refer (so that ref(A) equals ref(B)).

(Specialization: A of B)
(Specialization: B of A)

A co-reference mechanism is needed to "conflate" two entities which are discovered to co-refer after they have been created separately. In conjunction with the distinct flag, it can be used for asserting multiple distinct subcategorizations of entities. It can also be used to allow multiple correspondence assertions to model different role relationships between the sets of objects to which two entities refer.

Overall, the subtyping of assertions presented in this section increases the expressive power of the representation while maintaining the simplicity of memory structuring in terms of entities, specializations, and correspondences.

2.2. Representation of context

Context factors and context activation

Context information is represented, at any given time during processing, by a collection of context factors. Each *context factor* contributes to the context activation of a particular set of memory entities. This set of entities is the *scope* of the context factor. Apart from its scope, a context factor has associated with it a *significance weight*, this being a numerical value.

There are various types of context factor, each of the context factors present being an instance of one of these types. In general more than one factor of a given type can be present at any given time during the interpretation of a text. The type of a context factor determines the way in which the factor is managed, as discussed later. When a factor is created, it is given an initial significance weight which depends on its type. Subsequently, as the processing of a text continues, the weight of a factor is degraded, often by gradual decay, in a way which also depends on the type of the factor.

We can now give a precise definition for the notion of context activation, a measure of salience in context. The *context activation* of a memory entity is the sum of the current significance weights of the context factors within the scope of which the entity lies. Thus, at any point in processing, the relative importance of each entity is determined by the context factors which contribute to its activation score.

In the marker processing framework (Section 2.3), we can associate with each context factor a marker which marks all the entities in its scope. (One reason for doing things in this way is that the marker for a context factor can be indexed along with other memory processing markers, for performing searches with respect to context as described in Section 2.3 and Chapter 8.) The numerical weight significance of the context factor can be associated with its marker symbol so that the context factor weight can be altered without accessing the entities in its scope. The context activation of a memory entity can be calculated, at any given time, by examining the markers which are attached to it and summing the significance weights associated with them.

Examples of context factor types

The concept of a factor type which I have given above is, deliberately, very general; for example it does not place restrictions on which entity sets can be context factor scopes. Some concrete examples are therefore in order. These should give a better idea of how context factors can be employed to represent information that contributes to foregrounding entities during text processing. After listing the factor types implemented for the Capture system, I will suggest some other possible factor types which the context mechanism can handle.

Example factor types from Capture

The types of context factor implemented for the Capture system fall naturally into seven major types, some of which include more than one subtype. The classification into major types groups together types of factor which are similarly motivated, but it is not part of the context mechanism as such. The seven major types, and the way in which their scopes are determined, are as follows.

(1) Recency. There are three types of recency of mention context factor: the sentence factor type, the paragraph factor type and the text factor type. The scope of a sentence factor includes any entities which are mentioned explicitly in a sentence, or implicitly referred to by anaphoric expressions in that sentence. It also includes any other memory entities that are created as a result of interpreting the sentence. For example, assuming that the referent for *the machine* is 'P7700' in the sentence *Marconi manufactures the machine that is supplied by Smith*, then the scope of the sentence factor might be 'Marconi', 'P7700', 'Smith', and 'E1'; where 'E1' is a specialization of the predicate 'manufacture' which is created during the interpretation of the sentence. These entities will also be included in the scope of a paragraph context factor for the paragraph including the particular sentence. The scope of the paragraph factor is all the entities referred to so far in the paragraph or created as a result of interpreting the paragraph. Finally, for each text processed, there is a single text factor whose scope consists of the entities mentioned in or created by the interpretation of the text.

(2) Emphasis. The scope of an emphasis context factor is a single memory entity. Such entities are referents for noun phrases playing syntactic roles regarded as foregrounding the referent. (Compare for example with Sidner's syntactic marking, Sidner 1979.) Two types of emphasis factor were implemented in Capture. "Syntactic-topic emphasis" factors foreground topics of sentences in the passive voice, for example the referent of *machine* in *The machine is supplied by Smith*. "Be-clause emphasis" factors foreground the agents of certain be-clauses, for example *Plexir* in *Plexir is a manufacturer*.

(3) Processing-history. These context factors increase the context activation of entities which take part in memory processing. In other words a trace of memory processing is used as a context factor so that a side-effect of a memory entity's involvement in processing is that the entity is foregrounded. For example, a marker processing operation executed during the interpretation of a clause with the verb *manufacture* might generate a history of processing context factor with 'make1' in its scope; 'make1' being the sense of *make* of which the entity 'manufacture' is a specialization. These factors are especially relevant to

the process of choosing between word senses that have not occurred so far in the text (see Section 3.4). Fortunately, given the way in which context is represented in our marker processing framework, encoding traces of memory processing as context information is straightforward (Section 2.3). The inclusion of "processing-history" factors and association factors (see below) gives a "spreading activation" flavor to this aspect of the Capture system.

(4) Deixis. The scope of a deixis context factor is the set of memory entities for which the sum of significance weights from recency of mention context factors is higher than a preset system constant. Thus the entities in the scope of such a factor will have their context activations increased if they have been mentioned frequently and recently enough in the preceding text. (This type of textual deixis is different from spatial and temporal deixis factor types which were not handled by the Capture system.) The behavior of a deixis factor depends, in part, on that of other factors; this is also true of association and subject area factors (see below).

(5) Subject area. The subject area (or topic) type of context factor is designed to increase the context activation of those entities in memory which are considered to be related to a particular subject area. In fact, the scope of such a context factor is the set of entities in memory which are related to (in the sense of taking part in some of the same memory assertions as) a specified set of entities which are taken a priori to represent concepts that are central to the topic. For example, this set of "core" concepts for the "data processing manufacturers and suppliers" topic (one of the domains of discourse for texts processed by Capture) is taken to include the entities 'machine', 'supply1', and 'manufacturer'. The entities in the scope of a context factor for this topic might include 'machine/component', 'supplies/agent', and individual suppliers known to the system. The information stating that certain entities are central to a topic is itself represented by memory assertions.

(6) Association. The purpose of association context factors is to increase the context activation of entities in memory which are closely associated with entities currently in focus (cf. Grosz's use of "implicit focus", Grosz (1977) and Sidner's associated foci, Sidner (1979)). For this purpose an entity is closely associated with an entity in focus if it is above the foregrounded entity in the specialization or correspondence hierarchies, or if both entities take part in a

correspondence assertion in memory. There are two types of association factor: primary association factors and secondary association factors. The scope of a primary association context factor is the set of all entities which are close, in the above sense, to any entities which have context activations higher than a certain preset constant. The scope of a secondary association factor is all the entities associated with the entities in a particular primary association factor.

(7) Task. The task-specific (i.e. database creation) component of the Capture system also creates instances of a factor which are very specific to its particular application task, as I will explain in Chapter 7.

Other example factor types

Apart from the task specific factor type, it seems plausible that the types of factor listed above can all influence the interpretation of "static" descriptive texts, e.g. texts describing objects. Intuitively, however, it would seem that the types of factor used by the experimental system could also play a role in processing most other types of connected texts, e.g. stories, as well as simple descriptive ones. However, many of these other types of text are likely, in addition, to require context factors more closely related to the overall structure of a discourse. Let us therefore go on to examine some possibilities for such context factor types.

(1) Time and space. For texts in which spatial and temporal relationships are prominent, that is where temporal and spatial proximity affect foregrounding, it would seem appropriate to provide context factor types for temporal proximity to events being described, and for spatial proximity. For example, the interpretation of texts describing sequences of instructions for robot tasks would probably benefit from the introduction of these factor types.

(2) Goals and discourse purposes. For modeling conversational discourse, a type of context factor can be provided which increases the context activation of memory entities closely related to the participants' goals or to the communicative purpose of a segment of discourse. Such a factor type would be particularly necessary in human-machine dialogue, for example advice giving systems. (Compare with the discourse purposes of Grosz and Sidner 1985.)

(3) Agent associations. A more specialized kind of association context factor is one which foregrounds objects, plans, and events related to the agents taking

part in situations described by texts, for example the principal characters of narratives.

(4) Event sequences. Factors can be created which foreground the entities used for representing generic events in stereotyped event sequences of the kind which have been encoded as "scripts" (Schank 1975) and similar predictive discourse structures.

(5) Dialogue structure. Certain discourses, such as the task-oriented dialogues studied by Grosz (1977), have a structure which closely mirrors the structure of other knowledge, such as knowledge of a mechanical assembly task. As with event sequences, context factors can be generated to foreground entities which take part in substructures of the knowledge guiding the discourse.

Activating high-level factors

We can view different context factor types as being on a continuum with "low-level" (or local) factor types at one end and "high-level" (or global) factor types at the other. Of the example types which I have given above, processing history, sentence recency, and association are low-level types whereas subject area, event sequences, and dialogue structure fall at the high-level end of the continuum. (This distinction between different levels of context factor types is related to the one often made between cohesion and coherence.)

One important advantage of taking into account factor types of both categories is that the low-level factors can be applied to the problem of identifying relevant high level factors and choosing between them. An effective way of doing this is to monitor the context activations of entities (or "central" entities) which take part in the memory structures associated with high-level factors. In this way the low-level factors play a "bootstrapping" role, a point I will return to in Chapter 4.

Combining the two sorts of factor types guards against forcing the interpretation of a text into a mould dictated by a high-level factor. On the other hand the interpretation of a text in less structured discourses can proceed if necessary (especially with regard to resolving local ambiguities) on the basis of low-level factors alone. I will discuss such matters again in Chapter 4 when the context mechanism is compared with other models for context and focus.

My remarks about additional types of context factor for dealing with more complex texts than the simple descriptive ones handled by the experimental system are, of course, only speculative. Thus I have not indicated how such additional factor types would be managed, i.e. which text processing operations would create instances of them and how their significance weights would be degraded. The way in which the context factor types used by the Capture system are managed is described in Chapter 6.

The "context factor", encoded as a marked set and a significance weight, is used as a uniform representation for the different contributions to context listed above. The advantages of this uniform representation for the application and management of context information will become apparent from the discussions of application and management below.

Context application

There are two kinds of ways in which the information represented as context factors is applied. These are as "choice applications" and as "threshold applications". In choice applications context activation is used to select between memory entities or sets of memory entities. The two most important choice applications are reference resolution and word sense selection. In threshold applications a context activation threshold is used to define a focus space. This can be employed to restrict reference resolution searches, and to decide on the referents of plural noun phrases. It can also be used to identify candidate "anchors" for the scopes of association factors, and candidate "core" entities associated with high-level context factors.

In choice applications, context information is applied at points for which the interpretation system does not have enough specific information to select between competing entities. Alternatively the interpretation system may apply context in this way if it lacks more powerful reasoning mechanisms (for ruling out candidates by extracting more from the available information). In threshold applications, context information is used to locate memory entities which are currently highly salient, for such purposes as restricting search processing. In Section 2.3 it will be shown that the marker processing model allows the application of context thresholds to be computationally efficient even if the number of entities in memory is large.

The application of context to various interpretation problems is discussed in detail in Chapter 3, and Chapter 6 shows more specifically how this is done in the Capture system and gives illustrative examples processed by Capture. These chapters discuss applications which involve either or both the choice and threshold applications of context activation values derived from any combination of factors. We now address the question of when context factors are created and how they are managed during the interpretation of a text.

Management of context factors

The context mechanism is responsible for keeping track of the context factors present and their associated scopes and significance weights. The management of context information amounts to creating context factors and adjusting the significance weights associated with them. These are considered in turn below.

Creating context factors

If we accept the view that contextual information is not derived from one source but from many sources, linguistic and non-linguistic at once, then the question arises as to how we can arrange for factors to be created. In order to achieve this, each component of the language processing system can create factors whose types reflect the kind of information which the component handles. The context information contributed by a component is available to any other component wishing to choose between more or less foregrounded entities, and to restrict its view to entities currently in focus.

Since the inclusion of new factor types in a particular implementation does not complicate the control structure for applying contextual information, it is possible to implement simple or comprehensive models of context within this framework. Components can create factors when they are activated in order to fulfill some text processing function. This is possible regardless of whether these components perform their functions in a serial or interleaved manner.

For example, factors embodying foregrounding based on syntactic marking would be created by the parsing component, whereas factors indicating recency of mention would be created by the component which performed reference resolution. Furthermore, components performing an application task, for example document retrieval, can also create factors which influence how the application task is carried out.

The memory component can generate history of processing factors, association factors and instances of high level factor types. The ability to create context factors when performing text processing operations which make use of memory allows us to view interaction with memory as resulting in the accumulation of context information. The creation of processing-history context factors represents the most direct manifestation of this.

How the scope of a context factor is determined when the factor is created clearly depends on its type. For some types of context factor, e.g. emphasis factors, the text processing operation which creates a factor also determines its scope. The scope of the other context factors, e.g. association factors, is determined by the state of memory and the context information present at the time the new factor is created. The scope of a high-level context factor depends in part on fixed memory structures, but can also include specializations of the entities in these structures which have been created during text processing.

In Section 6.2 I will list the scopes of factor types created by the memory, interpretation and application-specific components of Capture.

Managing significance weights
When a factor is created it is assigned a standard significance weight according to its type. The way in which the significance weight is subsequently altered also depends on the type of the factor. For this reason the context mechanism must keep track of the types of all factors which are present at any given time. This information is consulted, for example, when the significance weights of factors of a specific type are degraded. The context mechanism is also responsible for removing factors whose significance weights fall below a certain threshold.

The context mechanism as such does not stipulate restrictions on how significance weights should be altered in a particular embodiment of the mechanism. A number of simple methods for altering weights suggest themselves. These include gradual decay as processing progresses, degrading factors of a specific type when specified events take place during processing, and lowering the significance weight of a factor to zero when another factor of the same (high-level) type is created. These three possibilities were all used (for different factor types) in the experimental Capture implementation (see Chapter 6 for details of the management of the significance weights of the factor types used in Capture). There are clearly other possibilities, for example ones which boost significance weights as well as degrading them.

Very different schemes for the management of context information were experimented with. For example, a mechanism was implemented in which memory operations could be explicitly parameterized by only a specified set of context factors. All factors were treated equally in this scheme, so summing the significance weights for an entity was replaced by counting the number of factors, from the specified set, foregrounding the entity. A variant on this mechanism was also implemented which allowed memory operations to be parameterized by the set of factors which were currently at the top of a "context factor stack". These mechanisms were finally abandoned because they greatly complicate the flow of control in a text processing system by requiring that multiple contextual environments should be tracked so that they could be applied as necessary. In contrast, context application in the main mechanism described happens automatically with respect to (all) the context information present at the time of application. One of the issues with which this research became increasingly concerned was to what extent this constraining but simple control structure is adequate for text processing. The more complex control structures for managing context information which were abandoned appear to be constrained in the wrong way. The fact that the facilities provided by these control structures could be implemented in terms of the simpler model for context management suggests, but this is only a conjecture, that they may not be necessary anyway.

2.3. Marker processing

In Chapter 1 I outlined why marker processing was adopted as the computational framework for implementing the memory and context mechanisms. In accordance with this framework the scope of a context factor is encoded as a marked set, i.e. a set of entities the elements of which are all marked with a symbol, or "marker", uniquely associated with that factor. The implementation of memory retrieval is based on performing set operations, again using marked sets of entities. (Some marked sets, cf. the processing-history factor type of Section 2.2, can be used for both purposes.) The model for memory retrieval is an adaptation of Fahlman's marker propagation model (Fahlman 1979); it is convenient for extracting information which is implicit in memory organized in terms of classification hierarchies. The simplicity of marker processing lends itself to possible implementations in terms of parallel hardware; instead of making proposals along these lines we will instead discuss, in Chapter 8, marker processing software techniques for efficient memory retrieval in context.

Encoding memory as a network

In the marker processing model, the structures in memory are viewed as a "semantic network". Since the term "semantic network" has, somewhat confusingly, been used in different ways by different researchers (surveys such as those by Brachman (1979b) and Ritchie and Hanna (1983) make this clear) some remarks are in order.

A possible characterization of semantic networks is simply the purely formal one, namely that all semantic network systems use a graphical notation to display that which is being represented. This is a weak characterization since all graphs can be expressed in non-graphical notations, and it has often been pointed out that there is nothing inherently semantic or knowledge representational about graphs.

I prefer and have adopted here the characterization of semantic networks which has to do with processing rather than with static description. This characterization is the widely held view (see e.g. Schubert et al. 1979) that the graphical aspect of semantic networks is a way of stating which parts of a representation are to be implemented as pointers so that certain processing operations can be performed on a knowledge base in a way which makes these operations computationally tractable. In the case of the computational framework for implementing our memory and context mechanisms these operations are marker propagations, which I will discuss shortly.

For historical reasons, however, I will sometimes diverge from the above stance in which semantic networks are purely a computational rather than a representational issue. This is because, although there may not be any representation devices common to all systems which have been labeled semantic networks, there are a number of substantive features (such as "roles" and "inheritance") which are addressed by many of these systems and which are relevant to the minimal representation scheme adopted by the memory mechanism (see Chapter 4 for a discussion of some of these other systems).

Deriving links from memory assertions

Memory entities are the nodes of the marker processing network derived from memory assertions. The edges (or "links") are compiled from specialization and correspondence assertions. A specialization assertion of the form

(Specialization: A of B)

generates a pair of links; a "specialization link" from B to A, and its inverse, a "generalization link" from A to B. Correspondence assertions of the form

(Corresponds: R1 to O1 as R2 to O2)

generate a collection of links, including a "role-link" from O1 to R1, an "owner-link" from R1 to O1, a "role-specialization" link from R2 to R1, etc.

The flags indicating subtypes of assertions are represented by indicators which are attached to the link records encoding the assertions. As mentioned above a network encoding of memory has some useful access properties. For example, in our case, we can without searching access all the entities immediately below a particular entity in the specialization hierarchy, or all the generic roles for all the correspondences in which the entity is the role argument. These access properties are used to implement the marker processing model.

Retrieval operations

Retrieval operations are performed in much the same way as Fahlman's marker processing model (Fahlman 1979). Marker processing is really just a way of performing certain set operations on the entities in memory. The entities in each set are marked using a symbol (a "marker"), occurrences of which are attached to the nodes which stand for the entities. Marker processing is performed by sequences of marking operations and searches. *Marking operations* specify the sets which are being operated on, and *searches* extract the results, and intermediate results, of retrieval operations; they locate entities which satisfy marking conditions and threshold conditions. (Threshold conditions related to the context mechanism were not part of Fahlman's model.) Fahlman describes many examples of this type of processing in detail, and since the flavor of marker processing performed on memory is much the same as that of Fahlman's work I will give only a simple example of a retrieval operation. Further examples of this kind of operation are given by McDonald (see McDonald 1981) who employed Fahlman's system for solving the problem of compound noun interpretation. Retrieval operations similar to those used by McDonald are discussed in Section 3.3.

An example of performing a simple operation involving an "intersection search" is the retrieval in focus of memory entities which are specializations of the entity 'doctor' and which also fill the role of 'committee/chairperson'. A marker, "M1" say, is used to mark all entities below 'doctor' in the specialization hierarchy. A second marker "M2" is used to mark role specializations of 'committee/chairperson' in the correspondence hierarchy. The results of the operation can then be extracted by performing a search for entities marked by both "M1" and "M2" which have context activations higher than the focus threshold.

The entity sets marked during the execution of retrieval operations are the sets which form the scopes of the "processing-history" context factors of Section 2.2. There is no need for an additional marking phase to represent the entities in the scopes of such factors since the markers used in the operations, for example "M1" above, can serve this purpose.

In practice, retrieval operations can become fairly complicated, since they often involve further marking and search operations in order to check whether, for example, the results include only most-specialized entities, or whether the properties have been inherited in a valid way (see Fahlman 1979). Because of this, specifying a large number of retrieval operations is simpler if it is done in terms of combinations of a smaller number of standard retrieval operations (of which there are around twenty in the Capture implementation). Four examples of such retrieval operations are given below.

(1) Find the common ancestors in the specialization hierarchy of entities E1 and E2.

(2) Find a most specialized entity C which fills the role R for entity O. That is, C is the inherited version of R with respect to O.

(3) Find an entity O which is the owner of R when R is viewed as a role specialization of the generic role G.

(4) Find the most specialized role-owner pairs in correspondence assertions which express the relationship between two entities E1 and E2.

These standard memory retrieval operations can be specified in terms of the marking operations and searches for sets of entities satisfying marking conditions. It may be possible to work out a "complete" set of such operations which would be sufficient for any retrieval request made to the memory mechanism, but this was not attempted in the present work. (The range of retrieval operations which were implemented for the Capture system was determined by the requirements of the interpretation component and the task-specific component for the system's test application.)

Marking operations

Since each of the sets of entities which take part in retrieval operations is a marked set, it is the range of marking operations which determines the kinds of sets which can take part in retrieval operations. Marking operations depend on the network of "links" (between "nodes" standing for memory entities) which are derived from memory assertions. Thus one type of marking operation, a "marker propagation", takes an initial set of nodes and traverses the network from these nodes following links of some specified type, and marking, using a specific marker, all the nodes on the paths which are followed. (In fact I will also use the term "marker propagation" to refer loosely to marking operations in general.)

A new marker is generated and used to mark all the entities specified by an operation. The marker processing model which we are adopting requires the following four classes of marking operations.

(a) Propagation marking which begins at a single entity and marks all the entities which can be reached from this entity via a specified link type ("link type" is used here to indicate a pair of argument positions of memory assertions, as explained above). Examples of this type of marking operation are

> (a1) Mark all the entities above the entity E in the specialization hierarchy.
>
> (a2) Mark all the entities which are roles, or roles of roles, etc., of entity E, where R is a role of entity E if there is a correspondence assertion of the form (Corresponds: R to E as - to -).
>
> (a3) Mark all entities which can be reached by role-specialization links from entity E, where R is an immediate role specialization of E if there is a memory assertion of the form (Corresponds: R to - as E to -).

(b) Propagation marking, parallel to (a), but starting from the set of entities which are marked with a specified combination of markers, instead of just a single entity.

(c) Marking across one step of links, where further arguments of the memory assertions involved can be specified to be marked with a particular combination of markers, for example

(c1) Mark all entities E1 which occur in assertions of the form (Specialization: E1 of E2 (instance)) where E2 can be specified as a particular entity, or as the set of entities marked with a particular marker combination.

(c2) Mark all entities E1 which occur in correspondence assertions of the form (Corresponds: E1 to E2 as E3 to -) where E2 is a specific entity and E3 is specified as the entities marked by a combination of markers.

(d) Marking sets of entities (using a new marker) selected according to existing markers and context activation values.

(d1) Mark all entities which are marked with all the markers in one specified marker set, but not marked by any of the markers in another such set.

(d2) Mark all entities with a specified marker combination which have context activations higher than a specified threshold.

Search requests

As explained earlier, the marker processing model requires performing searches as well as the marking operations just described. (Clearly some of these marking operations themselves require searches.) The basic search requests which must be handled are

(a) the (intersection) search for all entities which are marked by a specified combination of markers, and

(b) the search for entities with context activations higher than a specified threshold.

The other necessary searches are combinations of these which specify that the search should be evaluated in one of the following special modes.

-- An activation threshold parameterizes an initial search, but this threshold is lowered and the search repeated if the initial search fails to locate any entities.

-- If no entities are located which have all the markers in a combination, then the search should be repeated until a set of entities is located which have K-1 of the markers in the combination, no entities having K (or more) markers in the combination.

-- The number of entities to be selected is specified, and entities with the highest context activations are chosen if there are too many candidate results. Specifying the number to be "one" is the most common case.

These variants of the simple intersection and threshold searches are used, in particular, during reference resolution, which is a frequent requirement. An important special case of (b) above is when the threshold is set to the "focus threshold", a constant which specifies the required level of activation for an entity to be "in focus".

The computational efficiency of the marker processing model, and hence the language interpretation mechanisms which it supports, depends largely on how these searches are performed for a large number of entities in memory. In the absence of parallel hardware of the kind mentioned in Chapter 1, a serial indexing scheme has been developed. This scheme depends on indexing marked sets as described briefly below.

An indexing tree is built in which memory entities are the leaves, and the other tree nodes are clusters of entities and clusters of these clusters, etc. Whenever a node in this tree is marked, the node above it in the tree is also marked with the same marker. This means that it is possible to follow the marker from the root of the indexing tree to all the leaf nodes marked with it. A search for entities marked with specified markers and having a context activation greater than some threshold is executed as follows. The search proceeds by starting at the root node and only passing through indexing nodes marked with the specified markers and having a sum of weights (associated with context factor markers) which is greater than the specified threshold (see a diagram given in Section 8.1 for an illustration of such a search).

The efficiency of these searches depends, in part, on the clustering criteria used to group entities under the same parent in the indexing tree. The clustering method which gave the best overall performance in the implementation of the Capture system was one which closely mirrored the (natural) classification imposed by the specialization hierarchy. The indexing scheme is, in some sense, a natural computational extension of marker propagation because of the way indexing markers "propagate" up the tree. An analysis of the efficiency of the basic intersection algorithm, clustering criteria, and more complex indexing schemes is presented in Chapter 8. However the important consequence of the scheme for the language processing mechanisms is that access to entities satisfying marking and threshold conditions involves only a small amount of effort.

3
Solving interpretation problems

3.1. Using the mechanisms during interpretation

I would now like to consider how the mechanisms of Chapter 2 can be applied to solving three common language understanding problems: reference resolution, word sense disambiguation, and the interpretation of implicit relationships. These problems are considered to be basic to natural language understanding in general; the interpretation operations used to solve them are themselves thus assumed to be domain independent although they may exploit domain knowledge. A number of other interpretation operations which the mechanisms support, such as predicate-argument derivation for verb clauses, the interpretation of be-clauses, and prepositional phrase attachment, are also necessary for text interpretation (see Part II for a discussion of these with reference to the Capture implementation).

"Interpretation" here is taken (intuitively) to be concerned with making explicit the propositional content of language expressions and incorporating it into memory. It is therefore dependent on the current context and the contents of memory. This framework for language interpretation contrasts with the approach in which a text is analyzed according to a "text grammar" (see e.g. Correira 1980) resulting in some form of text representation which can stand alone from memory, since it results instead in the incorporation of new information into an existing knowledge base, and the creation of new contextual information.

One approach to the interpretation process is to apply the memory and context mechanisms to the structures produced by a parsing component (or "analyser") after it parses each sentence. Any analyser which handles the sentences of a text independently from one another cannot be expected to resolve all ambiguities and references presented by each sentence in the text. In this case the interpretation component applying the mechanisms has the responsibility for handling the remaining ambiguities and references. An important advantage of separating the basically linguistic sentence processing from the interpretation with respect to memory and context is that this allows these processes to be studied in a focused way. This was, in fact, the main reason why the design of the Capture system followed this approach as described in detail in Part II (an example of another system constructed along these lines is described by Grosz et al. (1982)). Furthermore this approach does not force the analyser to make decisions which should really take memory and context into account because it can pass alternative structures to the interpretation component.

Another possible approach to the application of the mechanisms of Chapter 2 is to integrate the application of the operations for solving interpretation problems into the parsing phase. For example, the mechanisms could act as an "oracle" to an all-embracing parsing process. The primary advantage of this kind of architecture is the potential increase in computational efficiency which can be gained by not considering some of the possible (syntactic) analyses of a sentence. The interpretation of the initial segments of these analyses will already have been ruled out, resulting in a more deterministic language understanding process. However, this approach presents difficult problems arising from the more complex control structure and from the danger of making decisions too early. Since the first approach is better understood at present, and was used in the experimental Capture implementation, I will, in general, be assuming that the memory and context mechanisms are to be applied after an earlier parsing phase has been completed.

3.2. Noun phrase reference interpretation

The resolution of definite references made by noun phrases is essential to any text processing system which seeks to exploit the information conveyed by texts. This is certainly true of tasks like story understanding and summarizing, the database capture task which the Capture system performs, and probably also true for tasks which might be able to do without "in-depth" understanding, for example translation.

I would now like to describe an interpretation operation which resolves the definite references made by various types of noun phrase by locating a memory entity, or a set of entities, which correspond to the noun phrase. The noun phrase types which can be handled include pronouns, definite noun phrases, compound nominals, possessives, and noun phrases with restrictive adjectival and relative clauses. Examples of these are

It is made by Marconi.
P7720 comes from *there.*
These machines are red.
The terminal manufacturer makes P9920.
The cost of *Mikota's peripheral* is 235.
Smith supplies *the blue machine.*
Jones supplies *the machine that is manufactured by Plexir.*

The context mechanism is used to disambiguate possible candidate referents when constraints derived from the parsing structures are not strong enough to identify a referent uniquely. An entity not mentioned in the preceding text, but related in memory to a mentioned entity, can still be selected as the referent of a noun phrase because of the presence of, for example, association context factors.

The application of context to reference resolution occurs after the constraints have been identified by the reference interpretation operation. This section is concerned with how the constraints on referents can be derived and how the output of this process is formulated as memory search requests. Configurational (i.e. primarily syntactic, see Reinhart 1983) constraints on co-reference are not derived by the interpretation operation, since it is assumed that these have already been encoded in the parsing structure produced by the sentence analyser.

Deriving constraint markers

The main constraints on referents are encoded in the request as markers. Each of these markers will have been used to mark a set of memory entities satisfying a constraint (see below for a description of the derivation of constraints). The marking involved in this process is either performed specifically for evaluating a reference interpretation operation, or may have been performed already by a different interpretation operation.

The memory search request is a request for an intersection search to be performed using the constraint markers, so that entities satisfying the constraints can be located. The information in the request other than the constraint markers is used to control the way in which the search is performed. In the request built by a reference resolution operation this information specifies that the initial search should be parameterized by a context threshold, that the constraints on the search can be weakened if they are too strong and no memory entities satisfy all of them, and that context should be used to limit the number of referents to the "number expectation" (explained below) which is encoded in the request. The request is evaluated (in the manner described in Section 2.3) so that the result of the request is a memory entity, or set of entities, which satisfies as many of the constraints as possible, agrees with the number expectation, and is the best choice with respect to the current context information.

Mellish (1980) uses a reference resolution mechanism which monitors the set of entities satisfying constraints which are derived from the text, some of them by inference. These constraints are accumulated until they are strong enough to identify the referent uniquely. Reference resolution in our framework is similar to Mellish's mechanism as far as the accumulation of constraints is concerned. It would also be possible to allow the reference resolution operation to take advantage of further constraints derived from inferences which are valid in the domain of discourse. For texts in general, and for the example texts processed by Capture, it is not possible to wait until the accumulated constraints identify a unique referent because this does not always happen. (This does tend to happen, however, in the mechanics problem texts processed by Mellish's system, presumably because in such texts the problem needs to be described without any possibility of ambiguity.) The focus mechanisms for definite reference interpretation which are used by Grosz (1977) and Sidner (1979) are discussed in Chapter 4.

The following are examples of how we can derive constraint markers from noun phrase construction types.

-- If the head noun sense in the noun phrase is a generic entity (such as 'block') in memory, then a constraint marker is generated by a marker propagation which marks all specializations (including role specializations) of this entity.

-- The constraint marker for pronouns is derived by marking the specializations of a generic memory entity which subsumes the entities to which the pronoun can refer. Other special anaphoric words such as *there* and *then* are treated similarly.

-- Verb cases (such as 'agent') specialized to the arguments of the verb of a clause (e.g. the argument entity 'agent/of/murder') can generate a constraint. The constraint marker propagates down the correspondence hierarchy from the specialized argument entity.

-- Restrictive relative clauses of the form *who loves Mary* provide a predication from which a constraint is derivable. The predicate-argument form of the predication translates naturally into a constraint on entities taking part in correspondence assertions.

-- The form of a constraint for a restrictive adjective depends on whether it is viewed as a property of other entities (using correspondences) or a class restriction (using specializations). The derivation of the constraint is similar to that for relative clauses in the first case and to that for generic nouns in the second.

-- Constraint markers can be generated as the result of relationship interpretation operations (see Section 3.3 below). These can be used to encode constraints based on specialized relationships implicit in a wide range of constructions, such as those containing possessives, compound nouns, or words such as *have* and *with*.

Reference resolution search requests

I will now present an algorithm for applying context to the resolution of singular and plural definite references after the constraints have been derived. The number expectation mentioned earlier can be "one" for singular noun phrases, and "many" or a specific number such as "3" for plural noun phrases. The noun phrase interpretation operation assumes that this number information has already been extracted from the structures produced by the parser. The algorithm is in fact the one used by the Capture system when it performs reference resolution.

Taking first the case where the number expectation specifies a single referent, an initial search request which is parameterized by the focus threshold is evaluated. Thus the search ignores entities which satisfy the constraints if they have context activations lower than the threshold, and also ignores entities which satisfy the threshold condition but not the constraints. If this initial search fails to locate any candidate referents, then a second search is made without the threshold condition. If more than one entity is located by either search, the context activations of the entities are compared and the one with the highest context activation is chosen. When the context activations of the two best candidates for reference are equal, a derived association factor is created (Section 2.2). If this in turn has no selective effect then the choice between the best candidates is made arbitrarily. Finally, if there are no entities satisfying all the constraints, context activation is used to select between the results of searches for referents satisfying the highest number of constraints.

If the number expectation specifies a plural referent then the procedure depends on whether the number of entities in the set being referred to is known. When this is the case the correct number of referents is chosen from the entities satisfying the reference constraints by selecting those with highest context activations. When the number of entities in the set being referred to is not known the following procedure is used. An initial search is made for a memory entity which satisfies the constraints as well as a focus threshold condition, and which has already been created to describe the elements of a set. Such an entity may have been the referent of another plural noun phrase or it may have been created as a result of interpreting a simple conjunction. If the search locates many such entities then the one with the highest context activation is chosen as the referent. If, on the other hand, no such entity satisfying the threshold condition is found, then a search is made for all (individual) entities which satisfy the reference constraints. The set of entities located by this search is taken to be the referent of the plural noun phrase, and a new entity subsuming its elements is created.

It should be clear that the memory and context mechanisms are capable of supporting more elaborate variations of this algorithm. These variations could handle some of the less direct cases of noun phrase reference interpretation. Here are some examples of these cases, which are probably within the capabilities of the mechanisms:

-- Reference to objects which not only have not been mentioned, but which are only implicitly present as part of inherited descriptions. For example the *keys* in *This Ford and its keys were abandoned on the beach.*

-- A more complex case of the above is examples such as the second *it* in *John gave his paycheck to his wife. Jack gave it to his mistress* (a variant of the so-called paycheck sentences). A possible solution is to regard such sentences as containing references to an entity which is a generic role rather than to distinct entities which are playing the same role in different descriptions.

-- Creation of instances of entities of known type, and their identification with named objects when the name is given as new information. A simple example of this is *Haddon collected a jug from Daui. This is P259.*

-- Definite noun phrases with *other*. The choice of entity satisfying the reference constraints could be the "second best" candidate, as determined by context, or a candidate closely associated with the "best candidate". An example is *The other spear comes from Woodlark.*

-- Reference resolution to cover generic entities. An example of a noun phrase for which reference resolution should return a generic entity is *the dodo* in *The dodo is extinct.* This case presents difficulties, however, because the situations under which reference to generics is appropriate are not well understood at present.

3.3. Relationship interpretation

Relationship interpretation operations are used to derive explicit relationships from language constructs in which relationships are implicit or vague. These types of language construct include compound noun phrases, possessive noun phrases, prepositional phrases using *with*, and certain *have* clauses. We will consider two forms of the relationship interpretation problem. These correspond to two modes of interpretation which will be called "reference" mode and "creation" mode respectively. These two modes, roughly speaking, reflect the given/new distinction. In "creation" mode, interpretation can lead to the creation of new memory structures, whereas in "reference" mode, the relationships recognized can be used for memory searches, e.g. for reference resolution.

There has been less work on relationship interpretation than on, say, reference resolution. However, the problem of determining implicit or vague relationships was addressed in natural language work at SRI (where it is classified under "basic pragmatic functions" (Grosz et al. 1982), and more recently by Steinacker and Trost (1983). Compound noun analysis (see e.g. Sparck Jones (1983a) for a discussion of the difficulties involved), is treated here as a special case of relationship interpretation. Processes for the interpretation of compound nouns have been investigated by McDonald (1982). The approaches adopted in these projects all depend on the use of a conceptual memory, or knowledge base, the relationships identified being chosen from among those represented in memory. In particular, McDonald uses the NETL knowledge representation language and marker processing for implementing his compound noun interpreter. The basic algorithm for relationship interpretation presented here is similar to the algorithm used by McDonald. McDonald augments his basic algorithm with heuristics for selecting between alternative interpretations, a function which is performed in our framework by the context mechanism.

Retrieval operations for relationship interpretation

Relationship interpretation operations result in either memory correspondence assertions or memory entities taking part in inherited correspondences. Relationship interpretation makes use of a number of memory retrieval operations for locating the relevant correspondence assertions. There are three basic memory retrieval operations for relationship interpretation:

Op-1. Find a specialization of entity A which is the owner in a correspondence assertion (or inherited correspondence) in which entity B is (or can fill) the role.

Op-2. Find a specialization of entity A which is the role in a correspondence assertion (or inherited correspondence) in which entity B is (or can be) the owner.

Op-3. Find a specialization of entity A which is the role in a correspondence assertion in which entity C is the owner, where C is also the owner in a correspondence assertion in which the role is a specialization of B.

Each of these three retrieval operations will in general return more than one result. Variants on these operations reflect (a) whether context activation should be used to select the most foregrounded candidates; (b) whether we accept only most specialized entities, achieving this by marking strictly up the hierarchies from candidates; and (c) whether the results from the three different types are to be combined or compared; I will discuss this option later on.

Because of the use of these operations in compound noun analysis, the arguments which were "A" and "B" above will be referred to as the "head" and the "modifier" respectively. The situations covered by the operations can thus be stated very roughly as follows:

Op-1. Modifier may fill a role of head

Op-2. Head may fill a role of modifier

Op-3. Head and modifier may fill roles of some entity

McDonald's compound noun algorithm (McDonald 1982) that was mentioned earlier concentrates on the cases covered by Op-1. In other words it depends on decisions designating which entities are "concepts" and which are "roles". Whereas in many cases (e.g. *plum pudding*) it seems "natural" for the modifier to be viewed as the "role", this is less clear in other cases (e.g. *product number*).

Construction types requiring relationship interpretation

The head-modifier pairs to which relationship interpretation can apply occur in various construction types. The following list indicates the modifiers and heads for a number of such construction types. In the examples the modifier is underlined.

-- possessive: *doctor's horse*

-- attribute: *boy with a hat*

-- nominal: *beer cask*

-- adjectival: *lidded pot*

-- have-complement: *girl who has a stepmother*

The result of relationship interpretation for a modifier-head pair in "reference" mode is a set of specializations of the head.

A procedure is needed for dealing, in "creation" mode, with situations where there is more than one modifier on a noun. These may be different types of modifier (in the general sense of "modifier" adopted here) as well as multiple nominal modifiers. The algorithm which was implemented for the Capture system repeatedly applied the operation for creating a new entity from a modifier-head pair so that the result of each application was used as the "head" in the following application. However, the problem of determining the order in which this should be done was not solved satisfactorily, even though a first approximation to this was tried. The algorithm proposed by Marcus (1980) for determining the structure of compounds is promising for solving this problem since it is well suited to the approach to relationship interpretation being described here, which would play the role of his assumed semantic function. The problem also arises in the case of multiple nominal modifiers in "reference" mode. But interpretation of "possessive", "attribute", and "nominal" modifiers can happen independently in "reference" mode. Each of these modifiers, if present, can be combined directly with the head of the noun phrase to produce a set of specializations of the head which are then used for reference resolution.

A brief explanation follows of how the memory retrieval operations, and the application of context, can be employed in the two modes. (See Chapter 6 for specific examples processed by the Capture system.)

Creation mode

When interpreting relationships in "creation" mode, the result of the relationship interpretation operation is a single (newly created) memory entity. Assume that the relationship is identified as corresponding to the role-owner pair *R*,*O*. In the case where the relationship has been identified by Op-1 (modifier may fill a role of head), the newly created entity is a specialization of *O* which takes part as the owner in a new correspondence assertion in which a specialization of *R* fills the role position. On the other hand, when the relationship has been identified by Op-2 (head may fill a role of modifier), the newly created entity is a specialization of *R* that takes part as the role in a new correspondence assertion in which *O* is the owner. The third case can be handled similarly with two correspondence assertions.

We can apply context to the choice of appropriate interpretations by comparing the context activations of alternative (pairs of) memory entities which capture the possible relationships, for example determining the relationship implicit in the nominal compound *computer maintenance* in the sentence *The success of the company depended on computer maintenance.* The memory entities from which a choice would have to be made, on the basis of context activation, in this example might be 'computer/application', or 'maintenance/of/machine'.

Reference mode

Relationship interpretation in "reference" mode is a search operation which does not involve the creation of new structures in memory. The three basic operations Op-1, Op-2, and Op-3 are applied, each of which returns a (possibly empty) set of specializations of the head. The union of these sets is returned as the result of the operation, unless all the sets are empty in which case the head itself can be returned (as the trivially most specialized entity). If the set of candidate specializations of the head is non-empty, then the reference resolution operation which initiated the relationship interpretation can mark the entities in this set with a marker to be used along with the other constraint markers in the reference resolution process. In other words, we can think of relationship interpretation in reference mode as a request to search for specializations of the head that embody the constraint indicated by the modifier.

When discovering implicit relationships for reference resolution in this way, it is not necessary to apply context directly, but instead relationship interpretation simply generates another constraint and context activation is only used for selection at the end of the reference resolution operation. Alternatively the context mechanism can be applied earlier in order to choose between alternative possible implicit relationships, and to use the best choice to generate a more specific reference resolution constraint marker. Although this second approach is more modular, it is less preferable because it risks making a wrong decision on the basis of a weak contextual preference when stronger reference constraints (derived from some other source) would have ruled out the incorrect reference.

3.4. Word sense disambiguation

Word sense disambiguation is as important a part of interpretation as reference resolution. It is a prerequisite to, or at any rate interacts with, finding solutions to reference resolution, structural disambiguation and relationship interpretation. A survey of some techniques for word sense disambiguation and arguments for its central position in the interpretation process are given by Birnbaum (1985).

Clearly we can assume that a syntactic parser will rule out certain senses on the basis of their syntactic categories. The remaining problem is still far from trivial as can be appreciated by examining the entries of a conventional dictionary. For example the Longman Dictionary of Contemporary English (Procter 1978), a learning dictionary, gives ten verb senses for *join* and five for *deal*, and seven noun senses for *club*. Syntactic subcategorization (see e.g. Gazdar et al. 1985) means that a good parser can rule out some of these as well, but a selection between many still needs to be made for sentences like

She joined the club, and

She dealt the club.

It is assumed that there is a memory entity standing for each of the word senses which we would like to distinguish during the interpretation process. As with reference resolution, we can split the problem of word sense disambiguation into two phases. The first phase relies on the memory mechanism to provide constraints based on the assertions between entities in memory, and the second phase relies on the context mechanism to select between alternatives satisfying the constraints imposed during the first phase.

Constraints on compatible senses

For the first phase, specialization and correspondence assertions are employed as a kind of generalized selectional restriction. In particular, this can form the basis for deciding which noun senses can fill the argument positions of particular verb senses, and which verb senses can take particular noun senses as their arguments. Asserting that a memory entity standing for a verb argument is a specialization of another entity places a selectional restriction on the noun senses which can fill this argument position. For example, by stating that the entities 'join5/object' and 'deal2/object' (the object arguments of specific senses of the verbs *join* and *deal*) are specializations of other memory entities with assertions like

(Specialization: join5/object of organization), and
(Specialization: deal2/object of playing/card),

we can rule out different noun senses of the word *club*. Marker propagations (passing through inherited specializations and correspondences if necessary) can verify that a particular noun sense is compatible with a particular verb sense argument.

Using selectional restrictions is, of course, a very old idea in computational linguistics (see for example Katz and Fodor 1963). The kind of information embodying the restrictions must be represented in our framework in memory because it is necessary for other interpretation operations. It is therefore not necessary for it to be duplicated elsewhere in the system, for example as lists of semantic primitives in lexical entries. Another reason for wishing to place this information in memory is that it becomes natural to allow restrictions like 'playing/card' in the example given above. Although this concept is fairly central to one sense of *deal* it would only be included with reservations, if at all, in many systems based on selectional restrictions. (The parser used by the Capture system itself applies selectional restrictions based on semantic primitives, so for this particular system the role played by the mechanisms in word sense disambiguation is mainly the contextual selection phase. See Chapter 6 for a discussion of this parser and examples of word sense disambiguation performed by Capture.)

Choosing between sense combinations

In a similar way to reference resolution and relationship interpretation, the second phase of word sense disambiguation depends on the context mechanism for choosing between the results suggested initially by the memory mechanism. Since word senses are just entities, choosing between two or more alternative senses of a single word is simply a matter of selecting the sense with the highest context activation. This simple action can therefore be taken if the syntactic and memory based constraints have eliminated multiple senses for all but one of the words in a sentence.

In the more general case, however, the application of the constraints results in a set of consistent word sense combinations. For example, it is conceivable that the first example sentence given above will still have two competing sense combinations:

join5 (enroll), club1 (society), and

join1 (cement), club3 (stick).

We can now take advantage of the numerical representation of context activation in our framework. We compute the sum of the context activations of the word senses in each combination and then select the combination with the highest sum. Compared with selecting senses for each word separately, this approach makes it less likely that correct senses will be ruled out because of small differences in context activations between the senses of a single word.

It is often possible to isolate word sense ambiguity, using syntactic information, to alternatives in a sentence substructure. A common case of this is nominal modifiers in compound nouns, where the head noun of a compound is unambiguous but its modifier is not. In this situation, there are two possible strategies for applying context in order to disambiguate the modifier. The first is to choose the modifier sense with the highest context activation and then perform relationship interpretation on the head-modifier pair. The alternative strategy is to use relationship interpretation to propose possible interpretations starting with the different senses and then select among these on the basis of context activation. However, it is not clear whether this more complex strategy would be more successful (and consequently the simpler first strategy was used in the Capture implementation).

The word sense selection operation which I described in this section combines techniques for lexical disambiguation used by some other researchers. For example it subsumes the association based technique described by Philip Hayes (1977b). This is because the context information on which disambiguation depends can combine the type of memory association information used by Hayes, in the form of association factors, with other types of context information (see Chapter 4 for a discussion of the importance of combining such factors).

Our approach to word sense disambiguation allows senses to be selected on the basis of contextual information the first time a word appears in a text. This is possible for two reasons. First, the method described above for examining context activations for combinations of senses means that a sense can be selected even if it has a context activation of zero (on its own). Second, the context activations of unmentioned word senses can rise when the preceding text has led to the creation of context factors, such as instances of history of processing, association, and subject area factor types. This is related to the problem (mentioned in Chapter 4 and Charniak 1982) of how the (American English) words *diamond*, *ball*, and *bat* are related to a "baseball" context when they all have multiple senses.

3.5. Other interpretation operations and some limitations

Apart from the three types of interpretation problem which I have discussed in this chapter the mechanisms are capable of supporting others such as

-- the derivation of predicate-argument structures for verbs

-- the interpretation of embedded clauses and be-clauses

-- structural disambiguation for prepositional phrase attachment.

The mechanisms offer less in terms of novel or elegant solutions for these other interpretation operations, but we still need to verify that all the interpretation operations can be performed by the same text processing system. Incorporating solutions to the various interpretation problems into the same system is an important issue for computational linguistics since it is often far from clear that independently proposed solutions to different interpretation problems are in fact compatible. The other operations just listed are thus still interesting from the point of view of how they fit into the overall structure of a system exploiting the memory and context mechanisms. For these reasons a discussion of other interpretation operations is given in Part II as part of the description of the Capture system.

Although the possible range of construction types discussed in this chapter, and those handled by the Capture system, constitute only a subset of English construction types, it is possible to extend this coverage to other, less common constructions, both by making the implemented operations more sophisticated and by including new interpretation operations (see Section 7.6 for some suggestions along these lines). However this still leaves a number of quite important language phenomena, representing a wide range of constructions, which cannot be handled by our framework. I will for now simply mention two categories of problem phenomena; those in the first category are judged to be more tractable than the ones in the second.

(1) Phenomena which can only be handled by complex (but probably feasible) extensions to the memory representation and interpretation mechanisms. These include negation, constructions conveying temporal information, and conditional constructions. Examples are

Smith does not supply this machine

The artifact must be from Daui unless she visited Keroka before 1890.

(2) Phenomena which would require new mechanisms to be incorporated in addition to those mechanisms forming the framework provided here. These include modality, simile, and metaphor. For example

The artifact probably comes from Woodlark but could be from Keroka

The spear head is like a razor.

In this chapter I have tried to show that the memory and context mechanisms can support an interpretation component with a good complexity/performance ratio; this being an important motivating goal of this research. For example, the interpretation operations applying context need not be aware of how the various factors that contribute to the context activation values at any given time were created, or how their weights were managed. The underlying reason for the choice of the three interpretation problems discussed is that the problems chosen result from common constructions that occur frequently. The aim was to demonstrate how a significant number of common interpretation problems can be handled in a coherent framework by the exploitation of the memory and context mechanisms.

4
Related research and a summary

We should now set this work in context by examining related artificial intelligence approaches in the areas of knowledge representation systems , and context and focus mechanisms for solving language interpretation problems. There follows a section on marker processing, and finally we close Part I with a summary of the mechanisms and the claims made for them.

4.1. The memory formalism

Artificial intelligence work on knowledge representation (and in particular semantic networks) has tended to be concerned with a number of issues which, while they have been considered central by many researchers, only cover a small part of the field. I would now like to examine how the design of our memory representation formalism compares, first to these issues in general, and then in more detail to two similar representation systems (NETL and KL-ONE) which influenced its design. For convenience in this chapter I will refer to the memory representation formalism used in our framework as "Memory".

Frames
Correspondence assertions are used to build structures in memory which resemble frames (Minsky 1975). Thus the "slots" S1, S2, ... for a frame F can be defined by correspondence assertions of the form

(Corresponds: S1 to F as ...)
(Corresponds: S2 to F as ...) etc.

Restricting the "fillers" of slots can be done by specialization assertions such as

(Specialization: S1 of E1).

The slot S1 itself may be thought of as a frame which inherits slots from E1, and similarly F may be a specialization of another frame E2 and inherit its slots. Frame F may also be a specialization of another frame E3, in addition to E2, allowing some notion of "multiple description" (see e.g. KRL, Bobrow and Winograd 1977).

Memory thus has much in common with knowledge representation languages such as KRL which are based on the organization of knowledge into frames, and structures built in Memory (for example the database descriptions explained in Chapter 7) are often frame-like. KRL was intended to be as complete a knowledge representation system as possible, and included, among other things, capabilities for procedural attachment. However, in the design of Memory, it was considered that although procedures might be valid memory entities, the code for implementing them and invoking them should be handled outside the memory component.

Logic based networks

Much of the research on semantic network formalisms has been concerned with combining semantic networks with predicate logic based formalisms (for examples see Schubert et al. 1979, Shapiro 1979 and Hendrix 1978). One motivation for this kind of work has been the goal of maximizing the expressive power of network based formalisms. However, maximizing expressive power was not a design goal for Memory, and there was no attempt at allowing arbitrary predicate logic expressions to be represented in this formalism. The simple extensional semantics of Memory assertions given in Section 2.1 provides us with a means of comparing Memory assertions with (simple) logic expressions via the extensional semantics for some first order logic.

A different motivation for combining semantic networks with logic is exemplified by the work of Deliyani and Kowalski (1979) in which semantic networks are regarded as providing an indexing scheme and a potentially useful strategy for guiding the search for a proof. (This is consistent with the attitude taken here that the importance of semantic networks, as networks, is largely a processing rather than a representational issue.) Such systems often use something analogous to the specialization hierarchy as a convenient means for the classification of objects and storing their properties in a non-redundant fashion. Hendrix's partitioned networks (Hendrix 1978) are a good example of this.

Partitioning and quantification

Hendrix's system brings up another issue, that of clumping together the nodes and links of a network into larger structures. Hendrix relies heavily on the use of a technique called "partitioning". This allows portions of the network to be placed in "spaces". Many of the uses of partitioning during processing are handled in Memory with marked sets of entities. In order to simulate some of the static representational aspects of partitioning correspondence assertions could be used as follows.

(Specialization: S1 of space (instance))
(Corresponds: E1 to S1 as space/node to space)
(Corresponds: E2 to S1 as space/node to space) etc.

S1 could then act as the "supernode" for the space, i.e. the node which can be used, in the representation, to refer to the portion of network which forms the space. This would not deal with cases in which the inclusion of memory assertions in spaces is significant. The latter would require an extension to the representation formalism in which assertions could be annotated by the name of a "handle-node" (see Fahlman 1979).

This extension may not, however, be necessary anyway. Thus Martin (1980) asserts that the use of role-based structures gives a more natural modeling of the phenomena which partitioning was designed to model; and these are of course handled by correspondence assertions in Memory. The phenomena include, in particular, the representation of certain types of quantification. Thus the suggestions made by Martin (1980) on how to formally represent various readings of quantified English expressions point the way to how we could represent certain difficult cases in Memory. These include the representation of sentence readings exhibiting the referential/attributive distinction, and the collective/distributive distinction. Martin also claims that an advantage of his proposed representation is that it allows for the representation of partial interpretations (which can be refined later) when the quantification structure is unclear.

Two previous formalisms

The approaches to knowledge representation mentioned so far share some properties with Memory. The two formalisms discussed below had a much more significant, direct influence on its design. These are Fahlman's NETL system

(Fahlman 1979), and Brachman's Structured Inheritance Networks formalism on which the KL-ONE system is based (Brachman 1978). Representational issues arising in the context of these approaches are discussed with respect to the design of Memory in the rest of this section. Readers not interested in these formalisms may wish to skip to Section 4.2.

The NETL design was intended to be as complete a knowledge representation language as possible, and one compatible with a marker processing scheme. The design of KL-ONE was more concerned with producing a "clean" but general semantic network representation for knowledge representation. Nevertheless, NETL and KL-ONE are in fact very similar as knowledge representation systems. Some of the differences in the details of these representations will become apparent in the comparison with Memory. NETL and KL-ONE are semantic network representations in which there are a limited number of node types and link types. Both representations are structured around a classification hierarchy for nodes representing concepts. The concept nodes in these hierarchies have associated with them descriptions which are built out of "role" nodes of various types and link types associated with these role descriptions. Concept nodes inherit the role-based descriptions of other concepts which are above them in the classification hierarchy.

Both NETL and KL-ONE are more complex representational formalisms than Memory. The reasons for this are first, as already noted, Memory was never intended to be a complete knowledge representation formalism, whatever that might be, whereas the designers of NETL and KL-ONE took completeness as one of their design aims. A number of issues tackled in NETL and KL-ONE were therefore ignored. Secondly, as will be shown below, loosening NETL's and KL-ONE's built-in ideas about what constitutes a "concept" allows some of the explicit primitives of these systems to be encoded, as needed, using Memory assertions. (More recent work by Brachman and others follows an approach in which a simple formalism of the kind proposed here can act as the "definitional" component of more complete reasoning systems such as KRYPTON (Brachman et al. 1985) and KL-TWO (Vilain 1985).)

The simpler ontology of Memory comes mainly from the abandonment of the strict classification of entities into concepts and roles. Fahlman's concluding remarks about the NETL representation include the following (Fahlman 1979, p.231): "There is too much difference between the base-node of a description and a role; role reversal should be a smoother process than it currently is." In Memory, depending on which correspondence assertions are being considered, we can view an entity as either a concept with its own roles or as a role in descriptions associated with other entities. This leads to a natural way of having "multiple views" of entities because of the lack of a single structure imposed by the representation formalism itself.

In fact the Memory knowledge base used in the experimental system still makes use of correspondence assertions to construct a predominantly "concepts and roles" view of the knowledge represented. There are two reasons for this. First, the knowledge base was originally constructed when there was a distinction between concepts and roles, and this way of thinking of the entities persisted after the translation into the later version of the representation formalism. Secondly, the concept/role distinction probably provides a pragmatic way of representing some kinds of information, although it should not be one which is made into an absolute which forces artificial distinctions, but rather a derived notion dependent on view.

Issues not tackled by Memory

As I mentioned earlier, a number of issues which were dealt with in NETL or KL-ONE were ignored completely in the design of Memory. Memory does not deal with negation except as provided by the *distinct* flag. Clearly, this is an important direction in which to extend the representation system. The easiest way to achieve this for Memory is probably to adapt Fahlman's **NOT flags which can be attached to certain assertions. There is no explicit provision in Memory for cancellation of inherited properties. In NETL *CANCEL links can be used to cancel inherited properties in order to allow for exceptions, for instance the case of a three legged elephant. But many of the operations using memory will work if properties are simply explicitly over-ridden at a lower level of the specialization hierarchy. This is an imprecise solution to the problem, but then cancellation links are themselves not problem free. The inheritance algorithm which takes cancellation links into account which was reported by Fahlman et al. (1981) was later shown to be inadequate. In KL-ONE (at least in some descriptions of the language) the taxonomy is taken as definitional (see below) and non-definitional information, like exceptions and cancellations, are considered to be best handled outside the representation formalism.

The defined class/natural class distinction was one which was dropped from Memory representation. One reason for this is that the memory mechanism does not make provision for maintaining the consistency of the knowledge represented, which would involve checking that entities of a certain type satisfied definitional properties, this being the main consequence for processing of the distinction between natural types and defined types in NETL. KL-ONE generic concepts are interpreted as defined terms and this is considered to be important for the classification of new objects and their incorporation into the knowledge base. Thus the natural/defined term distinction is closely related to the issues of consistency and the "digestion" of new information. (However, in some versions of KL-ONE (see Schmolze and Lipkis 1983) natural kind concepts are distinguished from defined concepts and then the classification algorithm must be told which natural kind concepts can be used to describe a concept being classified, because this information cannot be deduced.) Although these issues are important considerations for knowledge base systems, they were regarded as being beyond the scope of the minimal formalism provided by Memory.

Memory assertions for encoding NETL and KL-ONE descriptions

I would now like to describe the way in which a number of important NETL and KL-ONE link types are handled in Memory. It is not possible to say, formally, that a particular fragment of these representations is equivalent to a set of Memory assertions. This is because of the lack of a uniform semantics with which to compare them, or of any systematic indication of how the knowledge conveyed by certain English sentences in known contexts would be represented in the various formalisms. We must therefore base our comparisons on suggesting how the analogues of certain types of expressions in the other formalisms would be represented in a Memory knowledge base.

In NETL every *TYPE node T (representing a typical concept) has associated with it an individual node which represents the set, S, of entities which can be described by T. Properties of this set, such as its cardinality being equal to 4, can be associated with the individual node. This can be represented directly in Memory as follows

(Specialization: S of set (instance))
(Corresponds: S to T as set to set/member (uni))
(Corresponds: four to S as cardinality to set).

The semantics of these assertions permits the interpretation that the cardinality of ref(T) is 4, as required.

KL-ONE uses "ParaIndividual Concepts" (parameterized versions of concepts) in the descriptions of other concepts; for example a ParaIndividual of the SUPPORT concept is used in the description of the ARCH concept. In Memory there is no type distinction between an entity and the other entities (related to it using Memory assertions) which help to describe it. Thus although the SUPPORT statement in the arch description in KL-ONE is represented by a special node type (ParaIndividual), linked to SUPPORT by a PARA link, it would be just an entity specialization, 'arch/support' say, of the entity 'support' in Memory:

(Specialization: arch/support of support)
(Corresponds: arch/lintel to arch/support as supportee to support)
(Corresponds: arch/upright to arch/support as supporter to support).

Similarly the counterpart of NETL *IST (individual statement) nodes are (instance) specializations of entities which are specializations of the entity 'statement'. An example of an individual statement is the entity 'E20' below, representing the statement "Rockefeller owns Standard Oil":

(Specialization: owns/statement of statement)
(Specialization: E20 of owns/statement (instance))
(Corresponds: Rockefeller to E20 as owns/owner to owns/statement)
(Corresponds: Standard/Oil to E20 as owns/property to owns/statement).

NETL individual statements can be given a time-area scope which may be encoded by a correspondence assertion:

(Corresponds: 1890's to E20 as statement/time/scope to statement).

NETL has a special flag **PART which "Marks the PART *TYPE-role and all of its *TMAPS. Used to make PART-OF hierarchy operations more efficient" (Fahlman 1979, p.269). In Memory this flag is equivalent to a recorded marker propagation which starts at the entity 'part' (see Chapter 8 for a description of recorded propagations). There is also a distinction in NETL between two types of role ownership which are represented by *EXFOR and *EXIN links. Fahlman says that this distinction is reflected in English by the use of the prepositions *of* and *in*. However, it is not clear whether this distinction has any real value since NETL processing does not exploit it.

The KL-ONE language distinguishes between four different types of inter-role relationship. The assertions given below illustrate how these can be represented in Memory, or rather one of the ways in which Memory assertions can be used to do this.

(Corresponds: building/block to block/object as
physical/part to physical/object)
(Specialization: building/block of block)

(Specialization: arch of block/object)
(Corresponds: arch/block to arch as building/block to block/object)
(Corresponds: lintel to arch as arch/block to arch (uni))
(Corresponds: arch/upright to arch as arch/block to arch)

(Specialization: arch/1 of arch (instance))
(Corresponds: lintel/1 to arch/1 as lintel to arch)
(Corresponds: arch/1/upright to arch/1 as arch/upright to arch)
(Specialization: arch/1/upright/1 of arch/1/upright (instance))

The four different types of KL-ONE inter-role relationship are illustrated by this example as follows.

(a) The KL-ONE inter-role relationship "restriction", represented by a "modifies" link, is exemplified by the relationship between the entities 'building/block' and 'physical/part'.

(b) Differentiation, represented by a "differentiates" link in KL-ONE, is exemplified by the relationship between 'lintel' and 'arch/block', and also between 'arch/upright' and 'arch/block'.

(c) An example of "particularization" is the relationship between the entities 'arch/upright', 'arch/1/upright' and 'arch/1'. Here 'arch/1' is an individual arch and 'arch/1/upright' refers to its upright-blocks.

(d) The relationship between 'lintel/1' and 'lintel' is "satisfaction", since 'lintel' refers to the individual lintel for 'arch/1'. (It is unique because rel (arch, lintel) is a function.) The relationship between 'arch/1/upright/1' and 'arch/1/upright' would also be represented by a "sat" (satisfies) link in KL-ONE.

The relationship between Memory and the KL-ONE and NETL formalisms can be summarized as follows. All three formalisms make heavy use of a classification hierarchy for concepts which is also the basis of property inheritance between concepts. Correspondence assertions are used in Memory to provide a flexible way of modeling the relationships represented by roles in the other two formalisms. There are a number of issues, such as those related to consistency, which were considered to be outside the scope of a minimal system such as Memory. However, I have tried to show that the most important representational features of NETL and KL-ONE which depend on the various node and link types in these systems can be handled using the simpler Memory formalism.

4.2. The context mechanism

Implications of the context mechanism

Before discussing the context mechanism described in Chapter 2 we should first consider some implications of including it as part of a language processing system. The implications are for the application of context information in such systems, the class of texts which they can (in principle) handle, and more generally, for the management of context information in text processing. In order to avoid confusion the context mechanism belonging to our framework will be referred to in this chapter as the Context Mechanism.

In a system using the Context Mechanism it is not necessary to specify explicitly how the different types of context information interact during processing. Basically, it is only necessary to specify the language processing operations which cause the creation of the various factor types, and to specify how the significance weights associated with these types should be managed. After this, the context information present can be applied at any given point without regard to the types of factors which have been created. This simplifies the design of the system in that new types of context factors can be included without changing those parts of the system which apply the context information to interpretation problems.

The use of significance weights gives a simple way of comparing the relative importance of different types and instances of factors when context is applied. The use of numerical values in this way in AI systems may seem ad hoc, but it does have important advantages in certain cases, like the one of context presented here, because of the convenience of numerical values for comparing, degrading, and combining the effects of different context factors.

(For a discussion of the merits of the use of numerical values for a different purpose see Cater 1981.)

A separate issue is that the approach taken for applying context information can make the interpretation process more deterministic. Thus the Context Mechanism can act as an "oracle" which determines the path to be taken at choice points faced by the interpretation process. This leads to a more easily manageable control structure, since it is not necessary to keep a record of the alternative paths which were not followed, or to be able to decide when to backtrack and try other alternatives.

Further, building a context mechanism for deterministic language interpretation may result in a system which handles constraints on text structure naturally, for example constraints on the occurrence of referring expressions. Such a system would probably fail to process certain (misleading) texts correctly. (Cf. the claim made by Marcus (1980) that a basically deterministic mechanism for syntactic analysis can result in a grammar which elegantly captures generalizations reflecting constraints on sentence structure; and the expectation that a deterministic parser would fail to process "garden path" sentences.) The use of certain factor types can bias a system towards a deterministic interpretation control structure if they make it more awkward for the whole system to backtrack cleanly. In particular, "processing history" factors are (by their very nature) unavoidable side-effects of processing. In this case a backtracking mechanism would have to be able to save and reinstate information about the context factors present at any given point during processing.

A system which makes use of such a context mechanism for deterministic interpretation clearly cannot handle texts which do not satisfy the following condition: the "best" interpretation of each sentence with respect to the context provided by the preceding sentences is in fact the correct interpretation in the context of the complete text. Whether the Context Mechanism can always determine the "best" choice depends on how well the range of context factors and significance weights capture all the elements affecting the interpretation of text, which may be evaluated by agreement with human interpretation. It is not difficult to construct texts which do not satisfy the condition just given, i.e. which fool the interpretation process into making decisions which need to be revised because they are inconsistent with information supplied much later by the text. However, such misleading texts are rare and a technological approach to practical text processing, can, I believe, afford to ignore them for many applications.

A separate implication of the Context Mechanism is that it allows different components of the language processing system to contribute to the current representation of context by creating context factors (Section 2.2). This information is then potentially available to any other component which makes use of the knowledge stored in memory. Components creating factors can also manage the factors belonging to them by altering their significance weights.

This view of context, whereby loosely speaking it cannot be placed in a single box of a language processing system, possibly explains to some extent the difficulty of arriving at a foolproof characterization of what context is. The components of a natural language processing system often correspond to different levels of language analysis (syntax, semantics, pragmatics, etc.). Because of this, and because of the relationship between context information and the current focus, the above view of the management of context in a language processing system is consistent with the view of focus taken recently by Grosz, Joshi and Weinstein (1983), i.e. that it does not "yield comfortably to any account that is strictly a syntactic or semantic or pragmatic one".

The Context Mechanism provides the computational means for realizing this view of context in automatic language processing systems. Furthermore, the use of the indexing scheme for implementing "threshold searches" gives a computationally efficient way of accessing a constantly changing focus space even when the factors which contribute to context are managed independently by different components.

Comparison with other models for context and focus

As mentioned in Chapter 1, various context mechanisms can be viewed as means for restricting the use of a knowledge base for the purpose of taking context into account when performing natural language understanding. We saw in Chapter 2 and Chapter 3 how this view of context can be provided by the Context Mechanism in terms of the representation and use of information for constraining memory searches, and for selecting from the results of these searches. We will now compare the Context Mechanism with other models for context and focus.

In what follows I will first briefly discuss the use of context mechanisms based on scripts and related knowledge structures (Schank 1975; Tait 1982; Schank 1982a). Context mechanisms concerned with focus will then be considered (Sidner 1979; Wilensky 1982; and Grosz 1977). This work on focus is the most important for the evaluation of the Context Mechanism. Additionally, a "marker passing" theory of contextual influence (Charniak 1983) is discussed in Section 4.3.

Predictive discourse structures

Scripts, taken to mean knowledge structures which encode events in typical situations (see e.g. Schank 1975, Tait 1982), have been used to provide a strongly predictive context for processing texts by following the stereotypes encoded in the scripts. Thus a script is typically used to encode sequences of actions which occur in a certain type of situation, so that the understanding process can interpret a text, taken to be about this type of situation, by matching objects and events mentioned in the text against those expected by the script. The Context Mechanism is an attempt at producing a more flexible system which can deal with texts which do not fit any predetermined standard situation exactly. Trying to apply scripts to interpreting such texts can lead to errors because the predictions made by the script tend to take over the interpretation process; scripts can lead to disaster if the script chosen does not in fact fit the text at all (e.g. interpreting a news article in which *Pope's death shakes world* occurs as news about an earthquake which caused the death of one person).

I am not arguing that the use of knowledge structures concerning typical situations cannot play a role in the interpretation of a certain type of text (nor that, more generally, large memory structures should not be used by a context mechanism for text processing). The problem is that systems relying primarily on scripts tend naturally to rigidity as the penalty for predictive control of interpretation. Thus early script systems were clearly far too rigid; later script based approaches are either still too rigid or are sufficiently underdetermined to raise the problems which the original script idea was intended to overcome (cf. the remarks on MOPS below). In contrast, the less rigid use of context information by the Context Mechanism means that no single context factor can dominate the interpretation process to the point of completely distorting the propositional content of the text. The Context Mechanism is, roughly speaking, used to solve interpretation problems when they arise, rather than to predict the message being conveyed by the text.

As explained in Section 2.2 the Context Mechanism does not rule out the use of script-like information to implement "high-level" context factors which would be used to increase the context activation of memory entities in memory structures representing generic sequences of events. But this information would not be used in a strongly predictive fashion; it would have the advantage of being combined with information represented by other context factors, and hence would not dominate the interpretation. Another advantage of bringing scripts into this framework is that we can use context information derived from other factors to implement a reliable method of script activation (rather than, for example, keyword triggering, or pattern matching against sentence representations). We can do this by monitoring the context activation totals associated with the sets of memory entities representing the various scripts, and activating a script (i.e. increasing the activation of event entities in it) when the total associated with it exceeds a certain threshold, or, perhaps, when this is much higher than the totals associated with the other scripts represented in memory.

In more recent language understanding work, Lehnert et al. (1983) make use of MOPS to overcome some of the problems associated with the application of scripts to understanding narratives. MOPS are smaller and more generic structures than scripts, and can be combined in a flexible way with one another to form individual scripts ad hoc, as suggested by links ("strands") between different MOPS. Schank (1982a) claims that generalizing and merging the information present in many scripts and representing it in a non-redundant way as MOPS is a more realistic model of human memory organization. This approach is consistent with our memory mechanism where entities are not thought of as belonging strictly to large rigid structures but instead derive their meaning from the whole of memory.

The use of MOPS does seem to represent an improvement over scripts in terms of memory organization for natural language processing. However, it is not clear whether the systems in which MOPS are used have an adequate mechanism for deciding which MOPS to activate during processing. This is particularly true if the number of MOPS present in memory, and the number of "strands" between them, is realistically large. This is because in such a situation the MOPS activated lexically, or by following MOP strands, need not all be relevant to the current context. This suggests that it might be possible to activate MOPS by monitoring the context activation of the memory entities associated with them, in a scheme similar to that proposed above for applying the Context Mechanism to script activation.

Such a scheme may also provide a solution for the "frame activation problem" as stated by Charniak (1982). (In fact the use of subject area context factors in the Capture implementation can be thought of as an attempt at such a solution.) Furthermore, this solution seems to be capable of handling Charniak's "baseball" example, which he concedes cannot be handled by his own proposal for indexing on slots. Thus the context activations of (the appropriate senses of) *ball*, *bat*, *pitcher*, and *diamond* could be used to judge whether to create a context factor for the "baseball" subject area.

Focus based models

The Context Mechanism is more closely related, in its basic philosophy, to focus based mechanisms for interpretation in context.

Sidner's focus model

Sidner (1979) has developed a theory of definite anaphora interpretation (for English) which is based on determining the focus of a discourse; this is the entity on which the speaker centers attention, and which typically changes as the discourse progresses. The discourse focus is generally the preferred candidate referent for an anaphoric expression, and hence the knowledge-base element which is examined first during anaphor interpretation. More specifically, Sidner's algorithm for focusing keeps track of the current focus, an alternative focus list, and a focus stack. Focus can shift to an alternative focus if an anaphor cannot refer to the current focus. The focus stack records such rejected items, so that items on the stack can be considered after the list of alternate foci, if they prove unsatisfactory. Items that are associated with all these candidate entities are also considered as possible referents for anaphoric expressions. Association is defined with respect to information in a knowledge base which is assumed to be similar to Fahlman's NETL, and is similar to the information used for association context factors (Section 2.2).

Sidner provides detailed rules for the interpretation of various classes of definite anaphora, which indicate how the (discourse) focus, alternative focus list, focus stack, and associations can be used to interpret the anaphora. There are exceptions to the basic use of discourse focus which include a recency rule for processing certain pronouns, the use of an "actor focus" as well as the discourse focus, and co-present foci for the interpretation of anaphora such as *the one ....the other.*

These exceptions, and the need to keep track of alternative, associated, and stacked foci, dilute the notion of a single discourse focus of attention. This suggests that the use of context activation may be more appropriate since it does not make assumptions about a single (if shifting) focus of attention, but instead relies simply on relative context activation. Additionally, taking new context factors into account would require explicit detailed changes in Sidner's algorithms, whereas the algorithms used for applying the information provided by the Context Mechanism remain the same.

However, Sidner's work on definite anaphora comprehension is better motivated linguistically, and more sophisticated in its treatment of the various types of anaphora, than the reference interpretation operations described in Chapter 3. It is therefore worth considering how the insights of Sidner's work could be used effectively in a system depending on the Context Mechanism. In fact it appears that some features of Sidner's model (such as the effect of surface form on emphasis and foregrounding) could probably be incorporated as more sophisticated interpretation operations and context factor management; others would fall out naturally from the information encoded as context activation (such as the preference ordering for various categories of reference candidate).

The Context Model in UC

"Activation" is also used, to indicate foregrounding, in a context mechanism developed for the UC (Unix Consultant) system at Berkeley. The mechanism is an extension to PHRAN (Wilensky 1981) and is used by UC to support natural language dialogue for learning to use the Unix operating system. The mechanism (described in Wilensky 1982) maintains a "Context Model" which consists of a number of entries (entities, broadly defined) with associated levels of activation. Activation is used for what were termed "choice applications" in Section 2.2, in particular for some aspects of reference and word sense selection. Entries in the Context Model include assertions, objects, and representations which will be sent to other components (e.g. a discourse planner). When the PHRAN parser has analyzed a sentence, the results of the analysis are matched against entries in the Context Model, and new entries are added to the model. The entries are grouped into "clusters" representing associated fragments of knowledge, and increasing the activation of an entry causes an increase in the activations of entries in the clusters to which it belongs (cf. association factors). Activation decays over time, and entries with low activations are removed. There is also an indexed database of clusters from which clusters can be brought into the current Model when new entries indexing them are added to the model. In the reverse direction, a new cluster can be created from entries in the Model and placed in the database, where it is indexed by those entries which are most highly activated.

In UC, the current Context Model and the database of clusters have a combined function much like our memory mechanism: the entries in the Context Model correspond, roughly, to memory entities with context activations which are higher than some threshold. In the Context Mechanism it is not necessary to pull highly relevant items out of memory and keep them in a current context model because it is always possible, using the indexing scheme, to access these items efficiently and to restrict memory searches to them. This additionally means that memory assertions themselves can serve as associations (for the purpose of "spreading activation") so that it is not necessary to have a separate index from entries in a current context model to clusters in a database. The need in UC to create and index new clusters (which does not arise in our Context Mechanism) causes some problems (pointed out in Wilensky 1982). The UC system should be able to determine, on its own, when to create a new cluster (an operation which can be regarded as storing the current context). However the version of the UC system described by Wilensky (1982) must be instructed explicitly by the user to do this. A related problem is that the system cannot compare clusters and may therefore create more than one cluster each describing the same situation.

In the UC context mechanism there is no analogue of the "context factors" used in our mechanism for independent management of components of context activation. Again, the indexing scheme (described in Chapter 8) allows this generalization to be accommodated with efficient access to the most salient entities. However, the use in UC of an activation-based model for dialogue understanding indicates that this somewhat intuitive notion is useful in language processing settings different from those involving descriptive texts to which the Context Mechanism has been applied in the Capture system. Further development of both the UC context mechanism and the one described here may provide support for this claim.

Grosz's global focus

Grosz's work on focus (Grosz 1977) directly influenced the design of the Context Mechanism; thus the Mechanism can be thought of as a generalization of Grosz's "global focus" mechanism which is more widely applicable, and which tries to address certain problems brought to light by Grosz's work.

In Grosz's work focus information is used for resolving definite references made in task-oriented dialogues. The dialogue fragments studied were taken from conversations between an expert and a novice being instructed in assembling an air compressor. Focus is represented as a highlighted set of nodes in a knowledge base. This set is encoded as a "space" in the partitioned network formalism developed by Hendrix (1978). The focus space is taken from spaces in a partitioning of the knowledge base which mirrors the mechanical task of assembling an air compressor. Focus is used (Grosz 1977, p.5) to "differentiate among the items in the knowledge base on the basis of relevance", i.e. to select one space as salient so that nodes in this focus space are considered first as candidates for definite reference.

In what follows, I shall first consider the similarities between Grosz's focus mechanism and the Context Mechanism, and then the way in which the Context Mechanism is intended to extend and improve on Grosz's model. Grosz's immediate focus mechanism for ellipsis interpretation is a separate matter not of immediate relevance here, so I shall consider only her mechanism for global focus.

It has already been mentioned that the set of memory entities with context activations which are higher than a specified threshold can be thought of as the counterpart, in our framework, of Grosz's focus space. In fact, in the reference resolution operation described in Section 3.2 initial candidates for reference resolution are looked for in such a set of entities using the threshold search. If the search for referents in this set fails, the search is widened to memory entities outside it, just as the search for candidate nodes is widened to nodes outside the focus space in Grosz's case. In Grosz's model the focus space is augmented by giving precedence to nodes which are implicitly in focus, e.g. to subparts of those objects or participants in those events which are in focus. In the Context Mechanism, information on which implicit focus depends is utilized either explicitly in the form of association context factors or implicitly in the form of processing-history context factors.

Turning now to the developments made in our framework, it should be emphasized that the function of the Context Mechanism extends beyond the resolution of references made by definite noun phrases. It is applicable, for example, for choosing word sense combinations (Section 3.4). It is not clear exactly how Grosz's mechanism could be used effectively for performing this function because of the difficulty of guaranteeing that nodes corresponding to the correct word senses would be in focus (or implicit focus), since only nodes concerned with a stage of the assembly task would be in focus. Thus the form of the knowledge exploited for focus in Grosz's model limits the function of the model.

An advantage of the Context Mechanism's use of context activation is that the activations of arbitrary sets of entities, and in particular word sense combinations, can be added in order to choose between the sets. This can itself be used to trigger other factors to further sharpen context (Section 2.2). The analogue, in Grosz's focus framework, might be to count the number of nodes belonging to each set which are included in the focus space, but this would be less discriminating than summing context activations. Context activation can, of course, be used to choose between any two memory entities even when they are both included (or both not included) in the analogue of the focus space which is defined by a context activation threshold.

Another way in which the Context Mechanism extends the use of focus is that it is designed to allow the combination of very different types of context information. The type of discourse structure information which is based on the mechanical assembly task in Grosz's work could, in principle, be used as a "high level" context factor type (Section 2.2). This would imply a representation of the discourse structure information in memory in Grosz's style, with the subsequent creation of context factors increasing the context activations of subsets of the entities in the structures corresponding to the partitions used by the focus mechanism. The information represented by context factors generated in this way could then be combined with that from other factors in the usual way, contributing to the choice of referents for definite noun phrases.

The Context Mechanism also addresses a problem noted by Grosz which is associated with the important issue of how focus is shifted during the discourse. In her model shifting is heavily dependent on the structure imposed by the assembly task, and in fact Grosz points out (Grosz 1977, p.158) that "The major problem to adapting the focus representation to kinds of discourse other than task oriented dialogues is to augment the mechanisms for shifting focus... For such discourses, shifts in focus are often more gradual than in the task dialogues, and structural indications of shifts (segmentation) occur less often." On the other hand, the Context Mechanism provides a means for the gradual modification, through acquisition and degrading, of context information. New context factors are created as a side-effect of interaction with memory, and the significance weights associated with these factors are degraded as processing progresses. This results in the presence of many factors with different scopes, and a relatively smooth and gradual shift of the focus space defined in terms of a context activation threshold.

Using the context mechanism in other frameworks

We will now examine whether the context mechanism, viewed as a general AI technique for language processing, can be used in a variety of system architectures, in particular those which are different from the kind exemplified by the Capture system to be described in Part II.

The context mechanism is largely independent of many possible design decisions about system component relationships. Some of the suggested context factor types, in particular history of processing and association, depend, respectively, on the processing and representation models adopted for our memory mechanism. It is probably straightforward to design the counterpart of the association function for a different underlying memory mechanism, although making use of some trace of memory processing as a context factor type could prove difficult for different memory processing models. (This may be considered to be an advantage of the marker processing scheme.) In general, however, the use of context factors and context activation should be applicable to any systems in which there is something comparable to the "entity" of the memory mechanism. In particular, this does not rule out systems with logic based representation formalisms.

The context mechanism might also be useful in guiding the inference component of a text processing system. For example, it could be used in a system in which the inference component would generate all possible inferences by combining the results of language interpretation, with, and only with, statements in a focus space determined by context activation. Our aim would be to constrain the inferences made by the system (e.g. the system described by Cater (1981)) without missing those necessary for understanding. This type of context application is different from those discussed in Chapter 3 which can be characterized roughly as constraining a search through (semi) explicit information, as opposed to constraining the generation of new statements from existing ones.

It was mentioned in Section 3.1 that the context mechanism can be used for early interaction with the parsing component of a language processing system. Thus the context mechanism could be used to constrain, during parsing, the choice of word senses and semantic features to be associated with the referents of anaphora. Such a scheme would have disadvantages: for example, it is not clear to what extent it is safe to make use of constraints predicated by context before all the syntactic information in the sentence has been utilized (see e.g. Ritchie 1976). In addition, for most cases, this use of memory in conjunction with context to constrain parsing is simply an issue concerning efficiency (given, of course, that cognitive modeling is not being considered). Thus the incorrect possibilities considered by the parser, if it was not constrained, could be filtered out at a later stage by the other components (Woods 1973). Early application of context information would therefore only seem worthwhile for systems in an environment where the gains in efficiency were important enough to offset the associated risks of misinterpretation.

For language generation systems, the role of the mechanisms would be especially relevant to the choice of descriptions for objects and relationships. The specialization and correspondence hierarchies present a range of possible descriptions with varying degrees of specificity or generality (cf. the work by D. D. McDonald (1981)). The context mechanism would help in choosing the appropriate degree of specificity, and in determining whether to use modifiers, implicit or explicit relationships, pronouns or other definite noun phrases. For this purpose the context activations of the entities being described could be used both absolutely by comparison with predetermined thresholds, and relatively by comparison with other entities in memory to which candidate descriptions might refer.

4.3. The marker processing model

I will now make some remarks about the marker processing model with regard to related proposals for memory retrieval and contextual influence, and to computational efficiency.

Marker processing for memory retrieval

As mentioned earlier, the marker processing model is an adaptation of Fahlman's model (Fahlman 1979) to suit our memory formalism. In both these models, marker processing implements memory retrieval which extracts information implicit in a hierarchical classification. Our choice of processing model was partly motivated by the desire to investigate text processing techniques restricted by the consequences of having a processing model which could be implemented by parallel hardware of the kind proposed by Fahlman and others (see Hillis 1981). The parallel processing that might be achieved by such hardware is specialized, i.e. it does not aim at general concurrency, but only at performing certain particular types of retrieval operation very efficiently.

The adaptation of Fahlman's model to ours is determined by the types of marking operation which are allowed (Section 2.3). As there are differences in the memory formalisms (see Section 4.1) so there are corresponding differences in the possible sets of memory entities marked by propagating along "links" derived from memory assertions expressed in the respective representation formalisms. Clearly, such differences have more to do with the details of what can be represented in, and retrieved from, memory than with marker processing as such. However, the use of marker processing, in our framework, for handling the information represented by context factors is a significant difference. In particular, it implies a requirement for a larger set of distinct markers than Fahlman had assumed to be adequate; perhaps 100 distinct markers, rather than the 15 suggested by Fahlman.

Nevertheless, our marker processing model is still closer in style to Fahlman's model than to other related schemes, for example the marker processing algorithms proposed for KL-ONE (described in Woods 1978a) which make use of marker pairs. The very low level algorithms necessary to support the memory mechanism would also be different if retrieval was performed on a "connection machine" of the type proposed by Hillis (1981), because this would involve the use of "virtual links", rather than hardware links, between the processing elements which would correspond to memory entities. However, it might be possible to hide these differences in the "microcode" of the connection machine.

In contrast to general deductive retrieval, the processing model is only designed to enable the retrieval of semi-explicit information stored in memory, restricted if necessary by threshold conditions, to entities which are highly salient in the current context. Thus the model is probably not suitable for many artificial intelligence applications, for example one involving planning. Instead, the emphasis has been on having as simple a basic model as possible, and trying to build text processing mechanisms relying only on this limited form of access to a knowledge base. This is consistent with the simple, perhaps minimal, representation formalism.

One advantage of having such a simple scheme for memory representation and processing is that it is easier to specify what operations can be performed on the memory knowledge base. There have been calls (see e.g. Ritchie and Hanna 1983) for more formal specifications of the operations which can be performed with memory mechanisms similar to ours. I have not attempted to specify formally the operations that can be performed by the processing model; however, the first steps towards this have been taken by specifying the types of marking operation and memory search that can be used to implement retrieval operations. I have not specified, however, constraints on how retrieval operations may combine the available types of marking and search operation.

Marker processing for context

Charniak seems to have moved away from models of context based on frames towards one based on marker propagation (see Charniak 1983). This model has some properties in common with the Context Mechanism in that they both attempt to make use of NETL-like memory representation, and of marking to implement the model of contextual influences; however there are major differences.

Charniak's Marker Passing theory for context is one which is applied during sentence analysis (see Hirst and Charniak 1982), to assist the parser, with which it acts in parallel, to choose word senses and case-labels. It is mainly a mechanism for disambiguating word senses and case-labels only within the context of the single sentence in which they occur. The Context Mechanism, on the other hand, acts primarily on sentences taken together, and deals with interpretation problems which are unresolved at the sentence level using context information found outside the sentence.

In the Charniak and Hirst model, sense combinations are preferred if some connection between them is found in the memory network by passing markers in a way which is similar to their use by Quillian (1968). Charniak refers to this as "dumb marker passing", and suggests that it should be constrained somehow. Exactly how, however, is unclear since the theory described by Charniak (1983) had not yet been implemented. "Dumb marker passing" uses information which is analogous to that captured in the Context Mechanism as association factors and processing-history factors.

The common use of "marking" by these systems can, of course, be regarded simply as a characteristic of the computational aspects of these systems which does not say much about the linguistically relevant information which they use. However, this view is not totally satisfactory when we are considering the aspects of the Charniak and Quillian models (seen as cognitive science) in which the information manipulated by "dumb" marking is largely determined by the computational model itself. The Context Mechanism makes it convenient to use such information (as processing-history factors), but also allows components of the language processing system to create factors in a more controlled way and to control their effects more precisely by manipulating significance weights.

Software and hardware for marker processing

It is the simplicity of the marker processing model and the representation formalism which makes it possible, in principle, to implement memory retrieval on parallel hardware, or alternatively to take advantage of software techniques for improving the efficiency of retrieval operations. The latter option was followed here (see Section 2.3) using indexing techniques discussed in Chapter 8. If arbitrary functions were defined which could access memory representation structures directly, it would not be possible, without general purpose parallel hardware, to have a massively parallel hardware scheme, or to have a uniform indexing scheme which could be used for all software retrieval operations.

The advantage gained from the indexing techniques will depend on the particular knowledge base, the clustering method (Chapter 8), and, as with

McDermott's scheme for indexing Planner Databases (McDermott 1975), on the pattern of use. However, the programmer utilizing the marker processing model is to some extent freed from investing further effort in making individual search operations more efficient; Fahlman cites this as motivation for his parallel hardware design. It is difficult to estimate how successful the implemented and suggested techniques are for improving the efficiency of memory retrieval when the number of memory entities and assertions is very large. For the experimental Capture implementation, with several hundred entities and assertions, retrieval operations were performed efficiently enough, so the size of the memory knowledge base was not seen as a limiting factor. However, given that the techniques for improving efficiency are expected to be relatively more effective for larger knowledge bases represented in memory, it can be expected that these techniques would be quite adequate if the memory knowledge base was an order of magnitude larger than it was for the Capture system. If this turns out to be the case, then the use of software techniques should be adequate for applications in the near future, until specialized hardware becomes available. For natural language processing systems, however, the difficulty of constructing all the other components required for extensive coverage means that the lack of specialized hardware for memory processing is not currently the main limiting factor.

In any case, techniques for efficient simulation of specialized memory processing hardware are useful for experimenting with hardware designs. For example, as mentioned earlier, experience gained from implementing the Capture system suggests that the number of markers which can be stored at a node in Fahlman's design may be too small. (This is partly due to the way in which context information is represented with markers in our framework.) The use of software simulators is more important for evaluating more complex hardware designs such as Hillis's Connection Machine (Hillis 1981). The use of "virtual connections" in his design, instead of direct connections between processing elements, complicates the implementation of retrieval operations, and makes it more difficult to predict what the efficiency gains are for a particular application.

If it is accepted that context should play a role not only in disambiguation but also in enhancing the efficiency of a language processing system by limiting memory searches during the interpretation process, then care must be taken to ensure that the context mechanism is itself reasonably efficient. The incremental accumulation of information by the Context Mechanism requires a relatively small amount of computational effort at any point during the processing of a text. More importantly, the threshold searches can take advantage of the indexing scheme (Section 2.3) providing us with the means for applying context information, derived from many sources, to the enhancement of the efficiency of memory searches.

4.4. Summary of the mechanisms

Before moving on to details of the Capture system for database creation in Part II, I would like to give a brief summary of the mechanisms discussed in Part I, and the advantages they were claimed to have.

Mechanisms for supporting language interpretation

In Part I we proposed practical mechanisms for the representation and use of knowledge and context for automatic text processing. The overall design approach was that the basic mechanisms provided should be simple, well defined, and efficient, but at the same time flexible enough to deal with a wide range of common language interpretation problems and types of factor contributing to context. The mechanisms are not intended to solve interpretation problems which depend on complex reasoning for judging the relative plausibility of different interpretations derived from the text.

The memory representation formalism contains entities and two basic assertion types. Specialization assertions define a partial order which gives a classification of the entities in memory, while correspondence assertions classify the associations between them. Subtypes of these assertions can give more information about such classifications and indicate the functionality implied by particular associations.

The representation of contextual information (other than the context provided by the current contents of memory) is done uniformly in terms of instances of various types of context factors, the types reflecting different kinds of information which contribute to context. Each factor indicates that the memory entities in its scope should be foregrounded, or regarded as having an increased relevance, by an amount specified by the current significance weight of the factor. Factors are created by the components of the language processing system when they are invoked during the processing of a text. During language processing, a memory entity has a context activation value which is calculated from the context information present by summing the significance weights of the relevant context factors.

Both the memory and context mechanisms depend on marker processing as a computational framework. Memory retrieval operations are set operations implemented by marker propagations performed on a network structure derived from memory assertions. The scopes of context factors are collections of entities also encoded as marked sets. The main technique developed for increasing the efficiency of the memory and context mechanisms was the automatic indexing of marked sets, and hence the indexing of processing and context information. The indexing scheme can be used for efficient access to memory entities which satisfy specified marking and/or activation threshold conditions. In particular, this includes intersection searches which are restricted to a "focus-space" determined by a specified context activation threshold.

In Chapter 3 I showed how the mechanisms can be applied to solving three pervasive and hence important interpretation problems: reference resolution, relationship interpretation, and word sense selection. The memory mechanism provided the means for capturing constraints on solutions to these problems, while the activation values provided by the context mechanism allowed selection between alternative results of these interpretation operations to reflect the various components of the current context.

General claims about the mechanisms

The memory and context mechanisms have a number of identifiable advantages over previous proposals which influenced their design. The embodiment of the mechanisms in the Capture system lends support to the general claims made here, because it demonstrates that a system relying on these mechanisms is capable of performing non-trivial text processing.

The memory representation system has the advantage of being simpler than the representation formalisms on which it was based (the NETL and KL-ONE systems) while still retaining their most important features. This simplicity is important for ease of implementation and for the construction and maintenance of knowledge bases. The formalism still has a number of deficiencies in common with those on which it was based, such as the lack of facilities for a serious treatment of temporal information. Instead of trying to devise a "complete" representation formalism, we have devised a minimal formalism adequate for supporting many common interpretation problems. The other main advantage of the representation formalism, and one related to its simplicity, is that it can be given a well specified semantics. This allows a greater degree of confidence in using the representation, and gives a way of judging the validity of operations performed on it.

The advantages of the Context Mechanism as compared with others discussed in Section 4.2 can be summarized as follows. The mechanism provides a less rigid alternative to strongly predictive application of discourse knowledge structures. However, context factors derived from knowledge structures such as scripts or task-oriented discourse structures could contribute to the context information represented and hence to the definition of focus. Context information from other types of context factor can be used to "activate" such structures. The Context Mechanism has advantages over a number of focus based mechanisms for interpretation in context. In particular, it generalizes and improves Grosz's mechanism for global focus by allowing for the following: the application of context to a wider range of interpretation problems; discrimination between sets of entities and between entities outside the focus space; a gradual shift of focus; and the combination of heterogeneous context information, contributed by different components, in a uniform mechanism.

The use of marker processing as the computational framework for both memory and context shows how the mechanisms can be realized in terms of an inherently simple "spreading activation" model. As with other models of this type, traces of memory processing can provide context for disambiguation, but in our model this is easily combined with more carefully controlled context factors. As an alternative to suggesting a parallel hardware design for implementing marker processing, an indexing technique was developed for increasing the efficiency of software implementations of intersection searches for memory retrieval. The indexing scheme means that it is not necessary to keep salient entities separately from memory because it allows efficient implementation of activation-threshold searches even though the various context factors can be managed independently by frequent changes to their significance weights.

Much of the work in designing the memory and context mechanisms was devoted to trying to achieve a good "performance/complexity" ratio. In testing how far the simplicity of the mechanisms could be pushed, we discovered that a number of more esoteric features of memory representation and the application of context did not appear to contribute to performance and could be abandoned. Apart from being interesting in itself, the fact that the final simpler mechanisms can handle a wide range of phenomena means that they are well suited for incorporation into experimental systems that are investigating other aspects of language use.

Part II

5

Introduction to the Capture system

5.1. Language processing tasks

It is not easy to formulate a general definition for "understanding" natural language texts. In particular what an understanding system does in terms of drawing inferences and assimilating new information as a result of processing a text (or any other form of discourse) probably depends largely on the task for which the text was read. It is therefore appropriate, especially within the context of automatic language processing, to evaluate understanding with respect to a task to be performed as the result of processing a text.

The Capture system carries out a specific task, that of creating a relational database, as the result of the text processing that it performs. We will start by attempting to delineate the type of task processing performed by the Capture system as compared with that of some other experimental natural language processing systems. The description of the task-specific component of Capture, and the remarks made about other systems, are only concerned with that which happens (in the text processing system) before an external system (e.g. a robot, a database management system (DBMS), or an electronic mail system) takes over to actually perform the task itself. This "one-way" assumption is a limiting one, i.e. it excludes interaction between the language processor and the external task system during the latter's operations, but it is one which is commonly made.

The style of task-specific processing performed by Capture differs from a number of systems which have a similar application, i.e. generating a database from a body of texts. Two examples of these systems are those described by Sager (1981) and Cowie (1983). Sager's system uses sophisticated syntactic processing to produce tables from the processed texts, one application being the automatic processing of medical records. Each sentence is processed by a parsing component, a transformation component (which "regularizes" the parse), and then formatted by a third component into tables called "information formats" (in later work the tables are derived by flattening a "format tree" produced for the sentence). The last component uses rules which are specific to the domain being handled. These rules use syntactic information and a domain specific categorization of words in order to place each word from the sentence in one of the columns of the information format. For example, in medical radiology reports, there is a subcategory "TEST" of nouns which includes *film* and *X-rays*, and there is a TEST column in the information format so that the processing of *X-rays indicate metastasis* places *X-rays* into this column. The information format for a subject area is not an existing target database format, but is defined after analyzing syntactic and lexical regularities in a sample of the documents to be processed. Sager's system is thus not a database generator in the most commonly accepted sense of database (e.g. a strict relational model database). The formatted material generated can be described as a semi-formal database with a mixture of structural and textual elements.

Cowie's system processes descriptive texts about single objects. It uses keywords to identify parts of the object description (e.g. the keywords *flower* and *petal* for the flower-part of a plant description). It chooses fillers for attributes of these parts (e.g. *red* would fill the color attribute of the flower-part of the plant description) by checking property names attached to words in the dictionary (e.g. "vision-color" for *red*). Syntactic information is ignored, the text being split into segments at "pivotal points" such as conjunctions and punctuation marks. This design has several limitations, e.g. relevant information which is somewhat indirectly expressed may be missed, and the approach taken cannot handle text concerning more than one object or situation, since this would confuse, or simply merge, the information associated with the objects or situations described.

A related problem is that both these systems do not have satisfactory mechanisms for reference resolution, and so would not be able to process the examples handled by the Capture system, even though Sager's system does replace some of the words in the format tables with antecedents (also appearing in the format tables), and is therefore capable of handling some cases. Both systems make use of simple domain specific lexical categorization. This is not adequate for database classification of objects (described in Chapter 7) because one level of lexical categorization does not capture, for example, the (specialization) relationship between *machine*, *peripheral*, and *disc-drive*. In general, both Cowie's and Sager's systems can be viewed as template-filler processors, where the templates constitute a very minimal knowledge base, with rather weak control of the detailed character of the fillers, which are primarily text strings.

However, if other tasks are considered, then we can find many examples of language processing systems which make use of more interesting knowledge bases. One category of such tasks are those which are essentially linguistic in nature, for example translation, summarizing, and question answering. The systems described by Dejong (1979) and Tait (1982) use knowledge encoded in script-like formalisms in order to produce summaries of texts. The BORIS system (Lehnert 1983) uses a conceptual memory knowledge base organized in terms of MOPS, in order to achieve a depth of understanding which allows sophisticated question answering behavior after processing a short story.

The knowledge based processing in Capture is better characterized as not only directed at performing language processing, but also as using additional knowledge in order to perform an extra-linguistic application task. Examples of other systems which fit this characterization are the Consul system being developed at USC/ISI (see e.g. Mark 1981) and the natural language interface to a graphics system developed at BBN (see e.g. Brachman 1979a). Both these systems use the KL-ONE formalism for knowledge representation.

In the BBN system the PSI/KL-ONE interface (i.e. the interface with "Parsing and Semantic Interpretation using KL-ONE") was used to drive a sophisticated graphics display via natural language commands. In addition to encoding general conceptual knowledge about the objects being displayed (and referred to by the user) the task required encoding knowledge about how to display these objects. A "display expert" component used both the general conceptual knowledge and the display specific knowledge in order to drive the actual display. Attached procedures were used to generate "display form" concepts from object descriptions or from representations of commands to alter the display. The attached procedure mechanism was then used again to invoke "how to draw" procedures attached to the "display form" concepts.

The Consul system is designed to provide a cooperative natural language interface to interactive services such as an electronic mail service. The knowledge base includes concepts in terms of which users phrase their requests ("user knowledge"); knowledge about basic operations, such as "transfer", which can be used to describe services ("systems knowledge"); and specific knowledge about a particular service ("service knowledge"), such as concepts for transfer operations for sending different kinds of messages. The system uses rules, themselves represented in KL-ONE, for mapping user knowledge requests (created by the parser) into service knowledge structures which correspond to actually executable service operations. (If this is not possible, then the knowledge structures are used to explain why the user's request cannot be carried out.)

The framework chosen for application task processing in the Capture system is very similar to that of these two knowledge-based approaches. Thus the memory knowledge base used by Capture encodes language related, domain related, and task-specific knowledge, and also encodes the relationships which hold between them. In particular, the task-specific knowledge is independent from the language and domain related knowledge in the sense that memory entities and assertions representing the task-specific information (including further restrictions on the domain knowledge which apply in the context of the task) can simply be added to a memory knowledge base already containing assertions encoding the language and domain related knowledge. But the way in which control is organized in the task-specific component in Capture is different from the use of attached procedures, or the application of mapping rules for operating on knowledge structures. In Capture, the task-specific component uses the knowledge in memory via task-specific operations. These have the same properties as the interpretation operations used in the system, being procedures which interact with memory by the use of retrieval operations and the creation of new memory assertions. These task-specific operations are called at a number of specific points during text processing (see Section 7.5).

I will not argue that Capture's approach to application task processing is preferable as such to the approaches taken in the BBN and USC/ISI systems, since the motivation for the task component was rather different: the implementation of the database creation component of Capture was mainly aimed at verifying that a non-trivial application task could be performed (demonstrating, as suggested earlier, a certain level of language understanding) within the overall framework of the Capture system, based on the representation and processing techniques described in Part I.

5.2. The database capture task

"Database capture" is the task of processing natural language texts to extract that part of their propositional content which can be included in a structured database with a pre-specified format, the "target database". There are many possible applications for a system performing this task, such as the generation of relational databases from museum records and medical reports.

A text processing system for database capture can also be used, of course, by a human operator for the purpose of creating a database when no independent texts already exist. The question of whether or not writing texts for such a system is superior to some other user interface (e.g. an interactive form-filling system) was not addressed in this project.

It should be noted at this point that this task is distinct from that performed by the kind of natural language interface for database update discussed by Kaplan and Davidson (1981), and Maier and Salveter (1982). Their type of database update system would handle DBMS-oriented natural language commands such as *Change the status value for Smith from 15 to 30.* These systems concentrate on the interpretation of command verbs with respect to a given state of a database. The database capture task is concerned, instead, with processing paragraphs of text which need not have been written with a database in mind, and which do not make assumptions about the state of the database. However, it is easy to see that there is an overlap between systems performing the update and creation tasks: some updates could be formulated in a more natural way detached from the database management system. Most of the effort, by far, in building natural language interfaces to databases has gone into the design of natural language query systems (e.g. Woods 1978b; Walker 1978; Waltz 1978; Boguraev and Sparck Jones 1983; and many others). Much of this work has been concerned with interpreting the quantification structure of natural language questions in order to generate corresponding database queries, an issue which was not tackled in Capture. Clearly, however, natural language query systems are less suitable as an application task for investigating mechanisms for interpreting connected prose as compared with the database capture task (see below).

Database capture, in the sense defined, is considered to be a possible practical application area for the text interpretation mechanisms which were developed in this project. Thus the work reported here on database creation from natural language text is to a limited extent a study of the feasibility of such an application of automatic text processing. However, the main motive for choosing this task is its utility for testing our natural language processing techniques. The advantages of the database capture task in this respect are the following. Working with limited discourse domains in this application does not mean that we have made a simplifying assumption that is too unrealistic. The task requires the interpretation of language constructs in context in order to generate explicit database statements. This means that, in particular, there must be mechanisms for anaphoric reference resolution, and the resolution of sentence level word sense and structural ambiguity (i.e. ambiguities that are genuine at the level of single sentences). These problems associated with sentence level ambiguity are crucial to all text processing tasks.

Another advantage of the task is that we can make simplifying assumptions about the texts to be dealt with which cannot be made when performing other types of processing. For example, in-depth comprehension of narratives requires paying much attention to the goals and desires of the characters in stories. Having a test text type which does not require handling such complexities means that it is possible to concentrate on the more straightforward linguistic aspects of descriptive text, such as reference resolution and the derivation of the propositional content of descriptive sentences. Techniques for dealing with these latter issues are, of course, still relevant to processing narratives. Thus studying techniques for processing simple descriptive texts, such as the texts used for database creation, which are not concerned with human social affairs is considered to be worthwhile, and probably a necessary first step, before general text processing can be tackled.

The present system is not able to handle real, unedited, texts. This is because the coverage of constructions handled by its parsing component is not wide enough for this to be feasible (for example it cannot handle conjoined clauses), and also because of the small size, at present, of the system lexicon. In addition, the number and complexity of the language interpretation operations of Capture would have to be increased since the ones which were implemented cannot, and were not expected to, handle the full range of interpretation possibilities exhibited by descriptive texts (see Section 7.6). However, I believe that doing the work necessary to overcome these shortcomings within the framework, for memory and context mechanisms, of the present system could lead to a realistic system for database input for some very restricted applications, though it is certainly the case that the amount of work involved would be very considerable.

5.3. What the Capture system does

The Capture system is designed to perform the task of creating a database, with a specified structure, from the relevant factual content of a body of short English texts. Two example domains were used for testing purposes, and the memory knowledge base of the final version of the system contained assertions relevant to both domains. For one of these domains the texts used were records about a hypothetical museum's artifacts and their collectors; for the other the texts were thought of as retailers' records of data processing machines, suppliers and manufacturers. The target databases (the "Artifacts Database" and the "Machines Database") are composed of fixed format tables, of the standard kind conforming to the Relational Data Model. The relations and columns of these target relational databases are specified in advance.

The database capture task requires the implementation of solutions to common language interpretation problems in order that explicit database statements can be generated. For example, the processing, in context, of a sentence like *It is an arrow* requires determining the referent of the pronoun *it* and selecting the correct sense of *arrow* so that the following output (a "database creation statement") might be produced.

(ARTIFACTS/RELATION (ARTF/NUMB P670) (ARTF/TYPE weapon1))

Below are two texts from the example domains which were processed by the system, followed by the "database creation statements" which were produced for them. These statements can be used for incrementing the target relational databases; their detailed format is explained in Section 7.2, but here the relevant point is that they correspond to explicit statements, or propositions, derived from the texts.

Example text from the artifacts domain:

> Jones who was a trader collected P350 from Daui. He collected P370 from Woodlark. P350 is a necklace. P370 is an armlet. P391 is a necklace that comes from Woodlark. The condition of these ornaments is good.
>
> Armstrong and Haddon were British. They were academics. Haddon collected P597 and P598 from Daui. The artifacts are necklaces. The condition of these Daui necklaces is poor.
>
> P392 and P393 are armlets that were collected by Smith. This collector was a trader. The artifacts are fair.

Although this example text uses only simple English constructions, it demonstrates the way in which the system resolves plural definite references. For instance, the interpretation of the noun phrase *the artifacts* in the last sentence ultimately results in the production of the last two lines of the following output.

Database creation statements for the artifacts text:

```
((COLLECTORS/RELATION ((COLL/OCCP trader1) (COLL/NAME Jones)))
(ORIGIN/RELATION ((ORIG/ARTN P350) (ORIG/COLL Jones) (ORIG/PLAC Daui)))
(ORIGIN/RELATION ((ORIG/ARTN P370) (ORIG/COLL Jones) (ORIG/PLAC Woodlark)))
(ARTIFACTS/RELATION ((ARTF/TYPE ornament1) (ARTF/NUMB P350)))
(ARTIFACTS/RELATION ((ARTF/TYPE ornament1) (ARTF/NUMB P370)))
(ORIGIN/RELATION ((ORIG/ARTN P391) (ORIG/PLAC Woodlark)))
(ARTIFACTS/RELATION ((ARTF/TYPE ornament1) (ARTF/NUMB P391)))
(ARTIFACTS/RELATION ((ARTF/COND good1) (ARTF/NUMB P391)))
(ARTIFACTS/RELATION ((ARTF/COND good1) (ARTF/NUMB P350)))
(ARTIFACTS/RELATION ((ARTF/COND good1) (ARTF/NUMB P370)))
(COLLECTORS/RELATION ((COLL/NATN British1) (COLL/NAME Haddon1)))
(COLLECTORS/RELATION ((COLL/NATN British1) (COLL/NAME Armstrong1)))
(COLLECTORS/RELATION ((COLL/OCCP academic1) (COLL/NAME Haddon1)))
(COLLECTORS/RELATION ((COLL/OCCP academic1) (COLL/NAME Armstrong1)))
(ORIGIN/RELATION ((ORIG/PLAC Daui) (ORIG/ARTN P598) (ORIG/COLL Haddon1)))
(ORIGIN/RELATION ((ORIG/PLAC Daui) (ORIG/ARTN P597) (ORIG/COLL Haddon1)))
(ARTIFACTS/RELATION ((ARTF/TYPE ornament1) (ARTF/NUMB P598)))
(ARTIFACTS/RELATION ((ARTF/TYPE ornament1) (ARTF/NUMB P597)))
(ARTIFACTS/RELATION ((ARTF/COND poor2) (ARTF/NUMB P598)))
(ARTIFACTS/RELATION ((ARTF/COND poor2) (ARTF/NUMB P597)))
(ORIGIN/RELATION ((ORIG/COLL Smith1) (ORIG/ARTN P393)))
```

```
(ORIGIN/RELATION ((ORIG/COLL Smith1) (ORIG/ARTN P392)))
(ARTIFACTS/RELATION ((ARTF/TYPE ornament1) (ARTF/NUMB P393)))
(ARTIFACTS/RELATION ((ARTF/TYPE ornament1) (ARTF/NUMB P392)))
(COLLECTORS/RELATION ((COLL/OCCP trader1) (COLL/NAME Smith1)))
(ARTIFACTS/RELATION ((ARTF/COND fair1) (ARTF/NUMB P393)))
(ARTIFACTS/RELATION ((ARTF/COND fair1) (ARTF/NUMB P392))))
```

Example text from the machines domain:

> Plexir manufactures P9999 which is a computer. It is supplied by Smith. P1010 is a terminal that is supplied by Clark. This one is made by Mikota. These machines are red.
>
> P9000 is a green printer. It is made by Plexir. P4444 is a blue computer. The cost of the machine is 7850. The peripheral is supplied by the P9999 supplier. The terminal manufacturer makes the blue machine. The cost of Mikota's peripheral is 235.

Again, although the language used in this example is fairly simple, it illustrates cases of word sense disambiguation performed by the system, such as choosing the correct senses for *green*, *make*, and *terminal*. It also illustrates some cases of definite reference resolution.

Database creation statements for the machines text:

```
((MACHINES/RELATION ((MC/TYPE computer) (MC/MCNUM P9999)))
(MANUFACTURES/RELATION ((M/MNAME Plexir1) (M/MCNUM P9999)))
(SUPPLIES/RELATION ((SMC/SID Smith1) (SMC/MCNUM P9999)))
(SUPPLIES/RELATION ((SMC/SID Clark1) (SMC/MCNUM P1010)))
(MACHINES/RELATION ((MC/TYPE terminal1) (MC/MCNUM P1010)))
(MANUFACTURES/RELATION ((M/MNAME Mikota1) (M/MCNUM P1010)))
(MACHINES/RELATION ((MC/COLOR red1) (MC/MCNUM P9999)))
(MACHINES/RELATION ((MC/COLOR red1) (MC/MCNUM P1010)))
(MACHINES/RELATION ((MC/MCNUM P9000) (MC/COLOR green1)))
(MACHINES/RELATION ((MC/TYPE printer2) (MC/MCNUM P9000)))
(MANUFACTURES/RELATION ((M/MNAME Plexir1) (M/MCNUM P9000)))
(MACHINES/RELATION ((MC/MCNUM P4444) (MC/COLOR blue1)))
(MACHINES/RELATION ((MC/TYPE computer) (MC/MCNUM P4444)))
(MACHINES/RELATION ((MC/MCNUM P4444) (MC/COST 7850)))
(SUPPLIES/RELATION ((SMC/SID Smith1) (SMC/MCNUM P9000)))
(MANUFACTURES/RELATION ((M/MNAME Mikota1) (M/MCNUM P4444)))
(MACHINES/RELATION ((MC/MCNUM P1010) (MC/COST 235))))
```

Thus, apart from demonstrating that the system can carry out the database capture task, these example texts illustrate some of the capabilities of the system for language interpretation. The correctness of this interpretation can (usually) be determined by examining the output produced by the system. Although the language constructions used in these examples are of a very simple nature, the correct interpretation of these constructions frequently depends on the context in which they occur in the input texts, allowing the context mechanism to be tested.

5.4. Overview of how Capture works

The Capture system has five components which perform processing for:

(1) sentence analysis

(2) memory

(3) context

(4) interpretation

(5) database capture (task-specific)

The sentence analyser, or parser, is one developed independently by Boguraev (1979). The analyser passes information to the interpretation component; it is effectively a front-end to the core of the Capture system which is made up of the other components. The processing performed by these four components is interleaved. The context component is relatively small because the representation of context depends on memory (which we take to include marker processing for unimportant programming purposes), and because other components can take part in the management of context information (Section 2.2).

The analyser processes each sentence in the input text independently, producing a list of alternative analyses (i.e. parses) for the sentence. It uses an ATN (augmented transition network) grammar formalism and applies checks for semantic wellformedness on the structures which it builds, mainly by applying semantic category restrictions derived from Wilksian semantic formulae. The output analyses are dependency trees which use an extended set of case-labels to link verbs to their arguments and to exhibit the structure of noun phrases. By applying semantic checks, the analyser performs some word sense and structural disambiguation, but ambiguities that cannot be resolved using the essentially linguistic information which the analyser has at its disposal, and those which represent genuine alternative readings at the level of a single sentence, are presented as alternative structures in the analyser output, and must be resolved by the interpretation component.

The interpretation component uses the memory and context mechanisms to interpret the analyser output with respect to the contents of memory and the current representation of context information, i.e. with respect to information which might include specifying that a particular artifact is an arrow, and that this artifact is foregrounded in the current context. This component is implemented as "interpretation operations", the main ones being verb clause and "state clause" interpretation, predicate and argument derivation, be-clause and have-clause interpretation, noun phrase reference resolution, word sense and constituent structure disambiguation, and relationship interpretation for compound nouns, possessives, and function words. Collectively these operations perform the function of incorporating into memory new assertions that encode the propositional content of the input text.

Interpretation operations are procedures which, typically, are given fragments of analyser structures, and which use the memory and context mechanisms to perform a particular type of disambiguation, reference resolution, or creation of memory assertions. These operations also have the important effect of altering the current representation of context by creating new context factors. They can also invoke other interpretation operations, and in this way embody the gross flow of control in the system. For example, the evaluation of a clause interpretation operation may cause the evaluation of operations for noun phrase reference interpretation and for interpreting embedded clauses.

In order to perform their functions, both the interpretation and task-specific operations make extensive use of the memory knowledge base. This knowledge base includes assertions about both types and individuals. The knowledge base contains language-related entities such as noun and verb senses and case-labels; (world) entities in the domain of discourse, such as individuals and domain specific predicates; and task-related entities such as those taking part in the description of a particular relation in the target database. Just as important, the relationships between all these objects are also encoded in memory.

The task-specific component, or database capture component, is implemented by another set of procedures, the task-specific operations. These perform functions such as locating predicates in the database descriptions in memory, classifying entities with respect to the target database, and locating database names. Like the interpretation operations, the task-specific operations can also create new memory structures and generate context information. The task-specific component uses the results of these operations to produce the database creation statements. These should then be used by a database management system to increment the target database, although, in fact, the output of the system was not fed into a database management system because this last step was not considered to be sufficiently interesting, nor does it appear to involve any difficulties given certain assumptions (discussed later) about the database management system.

The main task-specific operations, which invoke subsidiary ones, are evaluated at fixed points during the interpretation process. Interpretation and task processing are therefore interleaved, but this happens in a rather fixed manner. The typical flow of control for a single sentence is thus roughly as follows. The sentence is analyzed by the parser, and alternative analyses are passed to the interpretation component. Interpretation operations call on the memory component to perform retrieval from the knowledge base and create new structures, and they alter the context information represented. They also invoke the task-specific component which uses the results of task-specific operations which it invokes to produce database creation statements corresponding to the sentence.

6
Applying the mechanisms in Capture

The first and second sections of this chapter describe information represented and manipulated in Capture by the memory and context mechanisms respectively. The rest of the chapter explains how this information is used to solve language interpretation problems of the kind discussed in Chapter 3.

6.1. Memory representation in Capture

In the Capture system the knowledge stored in memory is knowledge about the domain world, linguistic knowledge of a semantic nature, and knowledge related to the database creation text processing task, although no strong distinction between these types is maintained. Thus task knowledge is regarded in this system simply as specialized domain knowledge which is used by a task-specific component of the system, and semantic information about word senses is regarded as generic domain knowledge. Representing these different types of knowledge in memory allows the relationships between them to be expressed explicitly with declarative memory assertions.

Language and domain entities

The memory mechanism is exploited to process the output of the analyser (semantic parser) of the system. Hence we need to have entities for language related semantic objects which appear in the structures which the analyser produces. These include noun senses, verb senses and case relations. We also need entities to represent objects and predicates specific to the domain of discourse, and instances of these which occur in a domain. The relationship between language related entities and domain related entities is basically that of the generic to the more specific along the specialization and correspondence hierarchies. I will use memory structures for the "Machines Database" as examples. Examples of language related entities are given first.

There are no entities representing words, but only entities representing word senses; these originate in the lexicon used by the parser. For example there are two entities with names 'printer1' and 'printer2' for the two senses of the noun *printer* that occur in the lexicon; and we have

(Specialization: printer1 of human)
(Specialization: printer2 of peripheral).

(For irrelevant historical reasons, some word sense names in the lexicon do not have sense numbers.) There are also entities for verb senses: for example both 'manufacture' and 'make1' are found in the lexicon, and memory contains the assertion

(Specialization: manufacture of make1).

Entities for words as opposed to word senses could be created by assertions such as

(Corresponds: PRINTER to printer2 as lex/item to word/sense)
(Corresponds: MANUFACTURE to manufacture as
lex/item to word/sense).

These would be necessary for a task such as translation or paraphrase, but were not included in the implementation of Capture.

There are also entities for case relations like 'agent', 'object', and 'recipient', etc. These correspond to (and have the same names as) the labels which mark cases in the dependency structures output as "meaning representations" by the parser. These cases may be specialized to particular verb senses:

(Corresponds: make1/agent to make1 as agent to verb/statement),

and the specialized cases can, of course, be specialized further as in

(Corresponds: manufacture/agent to manufacture as
make1/agent to make1).

Domain related entities include individual objects and facts, and types of objects and predicates which are relevant to a domain of discourse. For individual objects and facts we have memory assertions like

(Specialization: P7000 of disc-drive1 (instance))
(Specialization: Plexir1 of Paris/manufacturer (instance))
(Specialization: E1 of manufacture (instance))
(Corresponds: P7000 to E1 as manufacture/obj to manufacture)
(Corresponds: Plexir1 to E1 as manufacture/agent to manufacture)

State predicates derived from properties such as weight and color are represented by entities such as 'weight/of' and 'color/of', for example

(Specialization: weight/of of measure/of)
(Corresponds: weight/of/possessor to weight/of as
    measure/of/possessor to measure/of)
(Corresponds: weight/of/weight to weight/of as
    measure/of/number to measure/of).

Domain based constraints on the arguments of predicate entities can be expressed by specialization assertions such as

(Specialization: manufacture/agent of manufacturer)
(Specialization: weight/of/possessor of phys/obj),

or by correspondence assertions, for example

(Corresponds: manufacture/obj to manufacture/agent as
    manufacturer/goods to manufacturer).

An example of a domain specific entity is 'computer/manufacturer', for which we would have the assertions

(Specialization: computer/manufacturer of manufacturer)
(Corresponds: computer to computer/manufacturer as
    manufacturer/goods to manufacturer).

Correspondence assertions can also be used to express relationships which encode domain knowledge, for example

(Corresponds: component to machine as part to whole), and
(Corresponds: data/storage to disc-drive1 as data/handling to peripheral).

Task related entities

In order to express the relationships between the domain entities and database administrative entities like the names of tables and columns in a particular target database, the database objects and predicates which are implied by record types in the database must be made explicit. These objects and predicates are in fact taken to be specializations of domain objects and predicates. The memory knowledge base used by Capture systems contained the necessary task-related knowledge for both the Machines Database and the Artifacts Database.

The target databases used are relational databases (see e.g. Date 1981) i.e. they consist of relations (tables) in which the columns range over values of a certain type, each row indicating that certain statements (the underlying statements for the relation) hold between the values in that row. The domain-database mappings for target databases are defined by creating generic entities for the description of a typical relation in a relational database and then by specializing this description to descriptions of the relations in the target database. The description of the generic relation for a relational database is represented in memory by the entity 'db/relp'. This has associated with it a number of generic database objects ('relp/dbentity') and statements ('relp/statement') and we have the following assertions:

(Specialization: db/relp of db/schema)
(Corresponds: relp/dbentity to db/relp as schema/role to db/schema)
(Corresponds: relp/statement to db/relp as schema/role to db/schema)
(Specialization: relp/statement of statement).

Note that the structures associated with 'db/relp' specify that which constitutes the description, in memory, of a relation in a relational database, rather than the description of some particular relation. 'db/relp' also includes entities for the name of the relation being described, and for generic entries ('relp/entry') in the rows of the relation

(Corresponds: relp/relation to db/relp as schema/role to db/schema)
(Specialization: relp/relation of relation), and
(Corresponds: relp/entry to db/relp as schema/role to db/schema)
(Specialization: relp/entry of db/entry)
(Corresponds: relp/entry/value to relp/entry as entry/value to db/entry)
(Corresponds: relp/entry/column to relp/entry as
entry/column to db/entry).

There are also other objects associated with the descriptions of relations, which I will describe in Chapter 7.

An example of specializing 'db/relp' to the description ('manufactures/relp') of the 'MANUFACTURES' relation in the Machines Database includes entities for the relation and column names:

(Specialization: manufactures/relp of db/relp)
(Specialization: MANUFACTURES/RELATION of relation)
(Corresponds: MANUFACTURES/RELATION to manufactures/relp as
relp/relation to db/relp)
(Specialization: M/MNAME of column)
(Specialization: M/MCNUM of column)
(Specialization: M/CITY of column),

and entities describing a generic entry in a row in this relation, and how this relates, for example, to the name of a database entity ('dbentity'):

(Corresponds: manufac/name/entry to manufactures/relp as
relp/entry to db/relp)
(Corresponds: manufac/name/value to manufac/name/entry as
relp/entry/value to relp/entry)
(Corresponds: M/MNAME to manufac/name/entry as
relp/entry/column to relp/entry)
(Corresponds: manufac/name/value to manufacturer/dbentity as
dbentity/name to named/dbentity).

There is simply one underlying predicate for this relation. It is represented by the entity 'relp/manufactures':

(Corresponds: relp/manufactures to manufactures/relp as
relp/statement to db/relp)
(Specialization: relp/manufactures of manufacture).

This is related to the database entities taking part in the db/relp. Thus we have, for example

(Corresponds: manufacturer/dbentity to relp/manufactures as
manufacture/agent to manufacture).

Not all "underlying predicates" follow this simple pattern; they can also be classifications of objects, e.g. for indicating machine types in the Machines Database, or they can be specializations of predicates derived from adjectives.

The examples given in this section should indicate how the relationships between linguistic entities such as word senses, and database entities such as column names, are expressed in Capture memory. The way the task related memory entities and assertions are used will be discussed later, when the database capture task is described in detail.

Before moving on from memory representation, it should be noted that the import of the "distinct" flag and the difference between the "rev" and "uni" flags are not always taken into account by the memory operations used in the Capture implementation. Thus the "distinct" flag is ignored by some operations, and others treat "rev" simply as "uni". Similarly, many of the implemented operations do not take specialization cycles into account. These limitations of the implementation do not cause the system to fail completely (e.g. to loop indefinitely), but do mean that some potentially useful information is ignored by the system.

6.2. Context factors and their management in Capture

In Chapter 2 the context factor types used in Capture were given as examples of possible factor types. Section 2.2 listed these factor types with an explanation of the sets of entities foregrounded by them. A summary of this information is given in the first two columns of the table below; the rest of the table summarizes the details, described in this section, of managing these factor types.

The set of initial significance weights for the types was determined by trial and error as the system developed and new test paragraphs were processed. When a new type of factor was introduced, an initial weight for the type was chosen intuitively, which was then increased or decreased according to the behavior of the system for the example texts. This was admittedly a fairly crude approach and indeed was not even based on any serious conduct of experiments. But in its defense, it should be said that attempts at more controlled experiments would have been inappropriate in any case because the example texts were written specifically for testing the system, and were not taken from an independent corpus of texts. As a result, no claims can be made about the real importance of the types of context information represented by the Capture factor types and about the way they are managed in the implemented system. Thus although the long term aim of the research is to develop computational systems which adequately handle linguistic reality, it has not been possible in this work to demonstrate conclusively that this is possible with the context factors employed in Capture.

A brief description is now given of the management of the various Capture factor types. The significance weights of many types are degraded using a standard degrading procedure. This applies to sentence-recency, emphasis, deixis, subject-area and association factors, while paragraph-recency factors,

Summary of Capture context factor types

factor type	entities foregrounded	when created	initial weight	degrading
recency (sentence)	mentioned in sentence	sentence processing	100	standard
recency (paragraph)	mentioned in paragraph	paragraph processing	50	end of paragraph
emphasis (intensive)	subject referents	certain be-clauses	90	standard
emphasis (passive)	topic referents	passive constructions	20	standard
processing history	entities in propagations (any)	memory retrieval	20	end of sentence
deixis	high recency weightings	"this" noun phrases	90	standard
subject area	associated with subject core-concepts	paragraph processing	60	standard
association (primary and secondary)	associated with highly active entities	ambiguity resolution	50	standard
task-specific	database relation descriptions	database predicate instantiation	180	end of task operation

processing-history factors and task-specific factors are not degraded using the standard degrading procedure. This procedure is as follows. At those points during processing when instances of certain context factor types (specifically recency and be-clause emphasis factors) are created the significance weights of all existing factors of the types mentioned above are divided by a system constant. This standard degrading ratio was 2 in the final version of the system, and integer arithmetic was used for convenience. After degrading factors in this way those with zero weights are removed from the system's records. It needs to be emphasized that degrading factors in a standard way are just details of how context management was carried out in the test Capture implementation; they are not regarded as theoretically motivated elements of the context mechanism as such.

(1) Recency
Sentence recency factors and paragraph recency factors are managed differently. Sentence recency factors are created by the "interpret-sentence" operation and given an initial weight of 100. The creation of a new sentence-recency factor causes a standard degrade to occur. A paragraph recency factor, with initial weight 50, is created by the "interpret-paragraph" operation. The weights of paragraph recency factors are degraded explicitly to 0 when a new factor of this type is created. The creation of a paragraph recency factor also causes a standard degrade on other factors.

(2) Emphasis
Be-clause emphasis factors are created by the "interpret be-clause" operation, and given an initial weight of 90. The creation of a be-clause emphasis factor causes a standard degrade. Emphasis factors relating to the syntactic topics of passive sentences are created by the operation for interpreting case fillers, and given an initial weight of 20; this does not, however, involve a standard degrade.

(3) Processing history
Since any memory operations can use memory retrieval which is implemented by marker processing, processing-history factors can be created by any memory operation. Such factors are given an initial weight of 20. The significance weights of processing-history factors are degraded by dividing them by 3. This happens at the end of processing a sentence. The weight of a recorded factor is incremented (also by 20) when a request is made for the propagation to be repeated; however, this is not a true incrementation: it is really creating a new factor.

(4) Deixis
Reference evaluation of noun phrases with deictic determiners generates a deixis context factor which is given an initial weight of 90.

(5) Subject-area
After comparing the activations of the "core" concepts specified in memory for the different subject areas, at most one subject-area factor is generated by the "interpret-paragraph" operation. It is given an initial significance weight of 60.

(6) Association
Association context factors are created by the operations for word sense and case structure disambiguation. They are also created as a result of evaluating reference resolution operations when the best candidates for reference have equal context activations. The two factors (primary and secondary associations) generated by any one of these operations are created before the selection done by the operation is performed so that the factors can affect the result of the operation itself. The initial weight given to each of the two association context factors is 50.

(7) Task
There is only one type of task-specific context factor in the system. The scope of such a factor is the set of memory entities describing a particular database relation (Section 6.1). This type of context factor is primarily relevant to the evaluation of some task-specific operations such as the extraction of the names of relational columns, rather than to language interpretation operations, although it can affect these latter operations indirectly. An example of a task-specific factor would have as its scope the roles of the entity 'supplies/relp', and the roles of these roles etc. The entities for column names of the 'SUPPLIES/RELATION' would be included in the scope of this factor. Database capture task factors are created by the operation which builds instances of underlying predicates for database relations. The initial significance weight given to such a factor is 180. The weight of the factor is degraded explicitly (to the initial weight of a processing-history factor) by the task-specific operation which generates database creation statements.

Further remarks on Capture context management

From the list given above we can see that the overall management of context factors in the Capture test implementation is as follows. The evaluation of text processing operations which interact with the memory component causes the creation of factors which, depending on their type, are either degraded uniformly at specified points during subsequent processing, or more directly by text processing operations managing them.

The Capture system does not take full advantage of the ease with which different components can contribute their own context factors (as discussed in Part I). For example the parser (being an independent subsystem which only generates analysis structures) does not create any factors. Thus, for example, (syntactic) emphasis factors which should really be created by this component are instead created (in a rather awkward way) by the interpretation component.

One of the considerations which had to be taken into account with respect to the management of context information was the overall activation of the entities in memory. In the implemented system the initial weights and degrading ratios ensure that after the first few sentences, the number of highly activated memory entities does not keep increasing. That is, the number of salient entities at a given time during processing is stable. Because of this, the various constant activation thresholds used by the system lead to roughly the same behavior as the processing of the text is performed. However, the introduction of new types of context factor in an extended system might require a more flexible approach which would allow system operation with very different overall activations of the entities in memory. One way of doing this, which was not investigated, might be to periodically reset the system thresholds to some fixed ratio of the sum of the significance weights of all current context factors.

In the process of trying to determine first approximations for managing the weights of the context factors, association factors seemed to cause instability, whereas exact management of the weights given to other factors did not seem to be necessary for stability. This may be because association is a rather loose and unstructured factor type. It might therefore be necessary, for systems using association as a context factor, to control the circumstances under which different degrees of association can be used profitably.

Apart from its direct application to solving interpretation problems, examples of which are given later, another way in which context activation is used during processing is in the generation of further context factors. Context activation thus plays a role in "bootstrapping" context information (Section 2.2). The scope of association context factors depends on existing context information. A context activation threshold search is performed to locate a set of "highly active" memory entities at the time the association factor is created, and the scope of the factor is determined from this set. Similarly, generation of subject-area factors is conditional on whether the entities in a predefined set concerned with that subject domain have, on average, sufficiently high context activations. What counts as a "sufficiently high" context activation for this purpose is determined by the size of the set concerning the domain, and a preset system constant.

6.3. Interpretation operations in Capture

I have already mentioned that the language processing framework used by Capture involves applying the memory and context mechanisms during the evaluation of "interpretation operations" which process the output of a sentence analyser (parser). The operations that were implemented are not an exhaustive list but they are sufficient for processing the example descriptive texts handled by the system. These examples, although much simpler than completely unedited texts, were not trivial and did provide instances of the requirements to be met by the interpretation component in sufficiently challenging forms. The interpretation operations for handling certain constructions are based on algorithms which are similar to the algorithms used by other AI researchers for handling these constructions. However, Capture integrates these various procedures into an overall processing framework in a coherent way by the common exploitation of the memory and context mechanisms.

Interpretation operations are implemented by procedures (in fact LISP functions) and as such are rather unrestricted. However, interpretation operations are intended to have, and do in fact have, many characteristics in common, the most important being as follows. Interpretation operations take as arguments structures produced by the analyser. The operations may evaluate other interpretation operations for processing substructures of their arguments, and then use the results of these subsidiary evaluations. The operations perform memory retrieval and context application using the marker processing model exclusively. They can create new memory entities, specialization and correspondence assertions, and context factors. The language interpretation operations embody the flow of control within the system as a whole. Thus an operation which interprets a certain type of clause can lead to the evaluation of other interpretation operations such as reference resolution, case specialization, and the interpretation of compound nouns and subordinate clauses. All of these imply memory and context processing.

At first sight it might appear that the interpretation of the analyser output is compositional in nature (i.e. that the interpretation of a structure is only a function of the interpretation of its substructures) because of the way in which the interpretation of structures uses the results of the interpretation of substructures. An example of a possible control sequence is one in which "interpret clause" calls "interpret verb case" which in turn calls "interpret noun phrase". But the interpretation of analyser structures is not in fact purely compositional because evaluating interpretation operations has side-effects which create structures in memory and alter the current context information. These side-effects can, in principle, influence the interpretation of other structures which are at the same level as, or lower than, the original structure in the analysis tree. Of course, an interpretation process can be considered compositional even if the relevant fragments of knowledge and context are left as parameters, or the results of interpretation are allowed to be functions of context, etc., so characterizing interpretation processes as being compositional, though a precise notion, can be misleading.

The various clause interpretation and related operations are described in Chapter 7 where I will also explain how task-specific processing fits into the Capture control structure. The examples discussed in the last three sections of this chapter will be those for which the memory and context mechanisms offer more interesting solutions to interpretation problems of the kind already discussed in more general terms in Chapter 3.

Since the analyser does resolve certain ambiguities, and its output does indicate some semantic relationships between sentence constituents, the basis for the interpretation process is initiated by the analyser. In order to obtain necessary background we will now look briefly at Boguraev's sentence analyser and the structures it produces.

6.4. The analyser and its output

The analyser is described in detail by Boguraev (1979; Boguraev and Sparck Jones 1982). It parses the sentences of the input text independently of one another. The analyser interleaves the use of syntactic information and semantic information (based mainly on semantic category restrictions) during the processing of a sentence. The control structure and grammar follow Woods's augmented transition network (ATN) formalism (Woods 1970).

The entry for a word in the system lexicon contains a list of word senses and the syntactic category information associated with them. Each word sense has a semantic definition which is a Wilksian semantic formula (Wilks 1975a). Such a formula is a binary tree of semantic primitives, although the rules for constructing a valid formula in Boguraev's system differ slightly from Wilks's original specification. The most important primitive in a formula is the "head" and this plays a direct role in applying semantic category restrictions. Also important are category restrictions on the fillers of verb sense cases and the "arguments" of prepositions. The restrictions are used to check the semantic well-formedness of structures being built by the ATN interpreter. This is done at points when major constituents are constructed, the most important of these being building the structure for a clause and building the structure for a noun phrase.

The output of the analyser for a sentence is a structure for each reading of the sentence, given that individual sentences may be ambiguous on their own (either absolutely or because the semantic power of the analyser is insufficient to resolve the ambiguities). The analyser output structures are case-labeled dependency structures for clauses, and are centered around the main verb sense. The case labels indicate a generic relationship between the verb and its arguments (or sometimes, a noun and its arguments). The labels are taken from an extended set of cases which include the more conventional ones such as "agent", "object" and "recipient", and others such as "mental-object". The case slot-fillers are either representations of noun phrases ("noun-args"), representations of adjective derived states ("state-args") or subordinate clauses with traces to the actual case fillers. Other information, about for example tense and aspect, is also included in the representation of a clause. (The detailed structure of noun-args and state-args will become clear when interpretation operations relating to them are discussed.)

An example of a complex analysis structure is the one below produced for *Smith who was a German trader collected P316 which is an arrow.* This structure indicates that the sentence was analyzed as a top level clause, *Smith collected P316*, with verb sense 'collect1' and two cases "agent" and "object".

The noun group structures for *Smith* and *P316* each fill the "agent" case of an embedded be-clause, *Smith was a trader* and *P316 is an arrow* respectively. The adjective *German* led to building an embedded "state-clause" (which is the same as the structure for *the nationality of Smith is German*). The semantic category primitives, e.g. "move" and "man", which follow noun and verb senses in these structures are ignored by the interpretation component because it has access to the more specific memory descriptions of the noun and verb senses.

```
(clause (type dcl) (tns past)
 (v (collect1 move
    (agent
       ((trace (clause v agent))
          (clause (type relative) (tns past)
             (v (be1 be
                (agent (n (Smith1 man)))
                (recipient
                   ((trace (clause v agent))
                      (clause
                         (v (be2 be
                            (agent
                               (n (trader1 man (det (a1 one)))) )
                            (state
                               (st (n (nationality NIL))
                                  (val (German1 kind)))) ))) ))) ))))
    (object
       ((trace (clause v agent))
          (clause (type relative) (tns present)
             (v (be1 be
                (agent (n (P316 thing)))
                (object
                   (n (arrow1 thing (det (an1 one)))) ))) ))) )))
```

The analysis structures can be regarded as "meaning representations" (see e.g. Sparck Jones 1983b), but for the purpose of the Capture project they are regarded primarily as data structures encoding linguistic analyses which need to be further interpreted with respect to the current context and the contents of memory. The structure of the Capture system allows it, in principle, to be able to process the output of a more purely linguistic parser (such as the structures used by Kaplan and Bresnan (1982) in conjunction with Lexical Functional Grammar). In this case some of Capture's interpretation operations would have to be made more complex and do some of the work performed in the present system by Boguraev's analyser.

6.5. Noun phrase reference interpretation

As explained in previous sections, reference resolution is performed as a subsidiary operation to clause interpretation operations. The constraints on reference which can be derived from a sentence are all applied at the point when a noun phrase is interpreted by Capture, the context mechanism being used to select between alternative candidates which satisfy the constraints. As explained in Chapter 3 the constraints are represented as marked sets. The following are examples of constraints derived from analyser structures.

-- For the phrase *the machine* for which the noun phrase representation produced by the analyser is

(n (machine thing (det (the1 one))))

all entities below the entity 'machine' in the specialization and correspondence hierarchies will be marked by the marker for this constraint.

-- If the head of the noun-arg is *it* then the marker used for this constraint will be the one which marks all entities below the entity 'inanimate' in the hierarchies. From the noun-arg (n (there1 spread)) in the analysis of *P7720 comes from there* a constraint marker marking specializations of 'where/ent' is included in the search request.

-- The 'agent' case in the analysis of *He supplies the disc-drive* is used, in the context of the Machines Database, to derive the entity 'supplier/dbentity'. Any entity that can be described as a 'supplier/dbentity' is marked by the marker for this constraint.

-- Nominal modifiers, such as *terminal* in *the terminal manufacturer,* and possessors, such as *Mikota* in *Mikota's peripheral,* are used to derive another constraint marker. This marker is generated by a relationship interpretation operation (evaluated in reference mode as described in Section 3.3).

-- Relative have-clauses, for instance the relative clause in *the machine that has the bolt,* and also noun phrases such as *the machine with the bolt,* are treated in the same way as possessives, so that relationship interpretation can be used to generate a constraint based on a more specific relationship than that suggested by *has* and *with*.

-- Constraint markers are generated for restrictive relative clauses such as the ones in *the machine that is manufactured by Plexir* and *the machine that is blue*. In the first of these examples the constraint marker marks the arguments of specializations of the entity 'manufacture' for which 'Plexir' fills the 'manufacture/agent' role. For the second example, the entities marked are arguments of specializations of the derived predicate 'color/of' that have the 'color/of/color' role filled with 'blue1'. Since the analyser representation for *the blue machine* is the same as for the second example, *the machine that is blue*, the predicate constraint marker generated is the same for both the adjectival noun phrase and the relative clause.

The "number expectation" for the referent (set) is derived from the noun phrase representation and included in the search request. This can be either an integer, or "many", i.e. an unknown number greater than one. The number expectation is "1" for singular noun phrases and "many" for plural noun phrases, for instance *the IBM machines*, which do not indicate the exact number of referents to be expected. This additional information is available when the determiner is *both* as in *both machines* in which case the number expectation is "2"; or when it is a number word, which is treated as an adjective, as in *the three machines*, giving "3".

I will now give some examples of reference resolution performed by Capture which illustrate the application of the context mechanism to this interpretation problem. (The numbers given for these texts are from Appendix A, which includes the final output generated by the system for the texts.) The algorithm used by Capture has already been explained in Section 3.2. Appendix B gives some examples of the effect of particular types of context factor when context is applied. The first two texts below contain instances of singular definite reference.

Text no. A18:

> Wintron manufactures P5050 which is a disc-drive. P1010 is a computer which is made by this manufacturer. It has a bolt. P8770 is a printer that is made by Plexir. Both peripherals are supplied by Clark. Smith supplies the machine with the bolt.

P4740 is manufactured by P5050's manufacturer in London. It is a micro-computer that is supplied by Jones. He supplies P8800 which is a terminal. The cost of the computer is 25. The computers are red. The three peripherals are green.

Examples:

-- The referent for *it* in *It has a bolt* is 'P1010' which is preferred over the other candidate 'P5050' because of its higher context activation.

-- Similarly, 'Jones' is chosen as the referent for *he* in *He supplies P8800 which is a terminal.*

-- The micro-computer 'P4740' is selected as the referent for *computer* in *The cost of the computer is 25* because 'P1010', the only other computer mentioned in the text, has a lower context activation than 'P4740'.

Text no. A20:

Plexir manufactures P9000. It is a micro-computer. Wintron manufactures P7000 which is a disc-drive. P9000 is supplied by Smith.

P8000 is a computer. It is supplied by Jones. The status of this supplier is 10. The status of P9000's supplier is 20. The micro-computer is red. The manufacturer manufactures P9090.

Example:

-- The referent for *manufacturer* in the last sentence of the text is taken to be 'Plexir', even though 'Wintron' was the last mentioned manufacturer.

The next three texts illustrate context application to plural definite reference, again using the algorithm described in Section 3.2.

Text no. A16:

P8080 is supplied by Peters. The status of the supplier is 20.

Clark supplies P7780 and P7790. P7720 is supplied by Robinson. These three machines are manufactured by Plexir.

Example:

-- A new entity is created as the referent for *machines* in *These three machines are manufactured by Plexir.* 'P7780', 'P7790', and 'P7720' are specializations of this entity. In the process of choosing three machines, 'P8080' was dropped because its context activation was lower than that for the other machines which were chosen.

Text no. A21:

> Haddon collected P33 which is an armlet. He collected P37 from Woodlark. It is a necklace.
>
> Bevan donated P571 and P352. P571 is a skirt. P352 is a necklace. Bevan collected both artifacts at Mount-Hagen.

Example:

-- The referent for *artifacts* in *Bevan collected both artifacts at Mount-Hagen* is taken to be 'P571' and 'P352'. The other artifacts mentioned, 'P33' and 'P37', have lower context activations.

Text no. A30:

> Jones who was a trader collected P350 from Daui. He collected P370 from Woodlark. P350 is a necklace. P370 is an armlet. P391 is a necklace that comes from Woodlark. The condition of these ornaments is good.
>
> Armstrong and Haddon were British. They were academics. Haddon collected P597 and P598 from Daui. The artifacts are necklaces. The condition of these Daui necklaces is poor.
>
> P392 and P393 are armlets that were collected by Smith. This collector was a trader. The artifacts are fair.

Examples:

-- The referent for *they* in *They were academics* is an entity which describes 'Haddon' and 'Armstrong'. This entity was created during the interpretation of the sentence *Armstrong and Haddon were British*, and it is chosen as the referent because it satisfies the threshold condition during the interpretation of *They were academics.*

-- The referent for *artifacts* in the sentence *The artifacts are necklaces* is taken to be an entity describing 'P597' and 'P598'. Although there is another entity (describing the artifacts 'P370', 'P350', and 'P391') which was created as a result of interpreting *The condition of these ornaments is good*, this entity did not satisfy the threshold constraint. The entity describing 'P597' and 'P598' has a higher context activation and satisfies the threshold constraint when the reference resolution is performed.

-- The referent for *artifacts* in *The artifacts are fair* is an entity which describes 'P392' and 'P393'. This satisfied the threshold constraint, and its context activation was higher than the entities describing the other groups of artifacts.

6.6. Relationship interpretation

In Chapter 3 we saw how the memory and context mechanisms can support the interpretation of implicit relationships present in various natural language constructions. The relationship interpretation operations described in Section 3.3 take a "head" and a "modifier" as arguments. These head-modifier pairs are recognized in analyser representations as follows.

(1) Possessives
The analysis for a possessive noun phrase such as *P777's manufacturer* is

```
(n (manufacturer man (poss-by (n (P777 thing)))) )
```

where 'manufacturer' is the head and 'P777' is the modifier.

(2) Attribute modifier
The analysis of a prepositional phrase using *with*, for instance *the machine with the bolt* is

```
(n
  (machine thing
    (attribute
      (n (bolt1 thing (det (the1 one)))) )
    (det (the1 one)))).
```

Here 'machine' is the head and 'bolt1' is the modifier.

(3) Nominal modifier
Simple noun-noun modification is represented in analyser structures without specifying which relationship might hold between the head and modifier. For instance the structure for *the computer manufacturer* is

```
(n
  (manufacturer man
    (det (the1 one))
    (nmod (((n (computer thing)))) ))).
```

(4) Ambiguous nominal modifier

Since the analyser does not do any (non-syntactic) analysis of noun-noun compounds, regarding nominal modifiers simply as a list attached to the head, it is not possible for it to select among possible noun senses corresponding to the surface noun modifiers. The analyser representation contains a list of the noun senses for the ambiguous modifier. For example the structure for *the terminal manufacturer* is

```
(n
  (manufacturer man
    (det (the1 one))
    (nmod
      (((n (terminal1 thing))
        (n (terminal2 spread)))) ))).
```

One of 'terminal1' and 'terminal2' is selected as the modifier (by contextual selection), 'manufacturer1' being the head.

There now follow some examples of relationship interpretation for simple modifier-head pairs, first in "creation" mode and then in "reference" mode. The retrieval operations used to locate candidate relationships are those we saw in Section 3.3, which were summarized as "Modifier may fill a role of Head" (Op-1), "Head may fill a role of Modifier" (Op-2), and "Head and Modifier may fill roles of some entity" (Op-3).

(a) Creation mode

The interpretation in "creation" mode of *computer manufacturer*, taken from the sentence *Plexir is a computer manufacturer*, say, proceeds as follows. A retrieval operation (Op-1) locates the relationship represented by the correspondence assertion

(Corresponds: manufacturer/goods to manufacturer as
organization/obj to organisation)

because it is possible for 'computer' to fill the 'manufacturer/goods' role of 'manufacturer'. Two new memory entities, E1 and E2 say, are created and then the following memory assertions are made:

(Specialization: E1 of manufacturer)
(Specialization: E2 of computer)
(Corresponds: E2 to E1 as manufacturer/goods to manufacturer).

The entity E1 representing the concept "computer manufacturer" is returned as the result of the interpretation operation.

Other actions might have occurred if the contents of memory had been different. For example, if the original correspondence assertion was not present, but instead, the following correspondence assertion was present and was located by retrieval operation Op-2:

(Corresponds: machine/manufacturer to machine as
goods/manufacturer to manufactured/goods),

then a new memory entity, E3 say, and the following memory assertions would be created:

(Corresponds: E3 to computer as machine/manufacturer to machine).

E3 would be the result of the interpretation operation in this case. The retrieval operation Op-3 is not used by Capture in "creation" mode, and so if neither Op-1 nor Op-2 had suggested any possibilities then the result of the operation would be just the entity 'manufacturer', i.e. the head. If Op-1 suggests one or more entities which could be owned by the head and at the same time Op-2 suggests one or more entities which could be filled by the head, then all of these entities are compared by the context mechanism, which selects one of them. The actions taken after this depend on whether Op-1 or Op-2 suggested the entity, and follow the pattern illustrated by the *computer manufacturer* example.

Finally, we consider an example of relationship interpretation in "creation" mode which is used to handle a *with* prepositional phrase. When interpreting the noun-arg representing *a pot with a lid*, 'pot' and 'lid' are the head and modifier respectively. Op-1 locates the memory correspondence assertion

(Corresponds: cover1 to container1 as part2 to whole).

This is located because 'lid1' is a specialization of 'cover1' and 'pot1' is a specialization of 'container1'. Two new memory entities, E4 and E5 say, are then created together with the memory assertions

(Specialization: E4 of pot1)
(Specialization: E5 of lid1)
(Corresponds: E5 to E4 as cover1 to container1).

E4 is the memory entity which is the result of the interpretation operation, i.e. it stands for the concept *a pot with a lid*.

(b) Reference mode

The interpretation of *the Mikota peripheral* can serve as an example, given that the following sentences have already occurred in the text being processed.

> Plexir makes P7770 which is a disc-drive.
> P9900 is a disc-drive that is made by Mikota.
> P9000 is a computer that is manufactured by Mikota.
> Mikota manufactures P9200.
> P9200 is a printer.

For *the Mikota peripheral*, the basic operation Op-3 searches for specializations of 'peripheral' that are the role in a correspondence assertion in which C is the owner, where C is any entity that is also the owner in a correspondence assertion in which 'Mikota' is the role. The correspondence assertions located by Op-3 in this case would have predicate instances which are specializations of 'make1' or 'manufacture' as their owners. The specializations of the head returned by Op-3 in this case are 'P9900' and 'P9200'. Similarly, the entities returned after interpreting *the peripheral manufacturers* would be 'Plexir' and 'Mikota'.

The interpretation of the possessive structure *Mikota's peripheral* would proceed in exactly the same way as that of its noun-noun compound equivalent illustrated above, again returning 'P9900' and 'P9200' as the possible specializations for the head.

An example which uses Op-1 is the relationship interpretation for *the machine with the bolt* in the context of a previous sentence such as *Plexir manufactures P7200 which has a bolt.* The sentence providing the context would have led to the creation of an instance of 'bolt1', 'E19' say, and the correspondence assertion

> (Corresponds: E19 to P7200 as machine/component to machine).

Op-1 searches for specializations of 'machine' which are in the owner position in which specializations of 'bolt1' are in the role position. This locates the correspondence assertion just mentioned and returns 'P7200' as a candidate specialization for 'machine'.

6.7. Alternative analysis disambiguation

The interpretation operations described so far assume that a single analyser structure has been selected for the sentence being processed. As explained earlier in this chapter the analyser produces alternative structures reflecting ambiguities with which it cannot deal. I will now describe the disambiguation operations of the interpretation component which choose between these alternatives.

The alternative structures produced by the analyser are usually whole sentence readings. (An exception to this, in which alternative substructures are indicated within a sentence representation, are alternative modifier structures for compound nouns.) The analyser produces such alternatives either because they correspond to valid alternative analyses at the sentence level, or because it does not have access to the (domain) knowledge which could be used for disambiguation. The operations described in this section handle three types of ambiguity exhibited in the output of the analyser; first, choosing between alternative analyses of a sentence that reflect word sense ambiguity; second, choosing between alternative senses for modifiers in nominal compounds; and third, choosing between alternative analyses of a sentence with different case relationship structures. These disambiguation operations depend on the context mechanism, and their main action is to derive the alternatives they are meant to handle explicitly and to present them in a form which allows the context mechanism to choose between them.

If two or more of the three types of ambiguity just mentioned occur in the analyser output for a sentence, then these are handled in the following order. The analyses are partitioned into groups which have the same word senses (ignoring for the moment multiple senses of modifiers in compound nouns). One of the groups is then selected using the sense disambiguation operation. The case structure disambiguation operation is then applied to this group of analyses to select one of them. This analysis is then interpreted by one of the clause interpretation operations, and this leads to noun modifier sense selection when ambiguous modifiers are encountered during the interpretation of the selected analysis. I will now give descriptions of the three disambiguation operations followed by some examples. Details of the influence of different context factor types for the texts in this section are included in Appendix B.

(1) Analysis selection based on word senses

The combinations of word senses present in each of the candidate analyses are extracted. For example, the combinations for the two analyses of *The printer is green*, which may be paraphrased as *The man who prints is a novice* and *The color of the printing machine is green*, are (be2 green2 printer1) and (be2 green1 printer2) respectively. A score is calculated for each of the combinations. This score comes from the context activation for the senses (as provided by the context mechanism) with an additional bias weight for senses which do have memory entities. The bias is introduced so that senses with memory entities associated with them are preferred over those without any, even when there is no context information attached to the memory entities. The result of the operation is simply the analysis (or set of analyses) for which the sense combination has the highest score. If more than one of the combinations share the highest score, then one of these would be chosen at random.

(2) Selection of noun modifier senses

As mentioned above, the analyser does not produce alternative sentence analyses for readings with different possibilities for the senses of noun modifiers in compound noun phrases. Instead, the alternatives are presented as a substructure of a single sentence representation (see Tait and Sparck Jones 1983). This substructure only indicates the order in which nominal modifiers occurred in the surface sentence and a list of noun senses for each of them. This is because the analyser does not have available to it the knowledge needed to determine the structure and meaning of noun-noun compounds. An example is listing the two senses of *terminal* in the structure for *the terminal manufacturer* (which was given earlier). The modifier sense disambiguation operation simply selects, from the list of senses for each modifier, the sense that has the highest context activation as provided by the context mechanism. The following two texts processed by Capture contain examples of word sense disambiguation.

Text no. A33:

> P900 is a spear. P700 is an armlet. This artifact was collected in Daui. It is common. The weapon was collected from there. P940 and P950 are arrows. P200 is a spear blade.

Examples:

-- Two analyses are produced for *P940 and P950 are arrows* with different senses for *arrow*. The analysis containing the sense 'arrow1' (a weapon) is preferred over the analysis containing 'arrow2' (a sign) because of the higher context activation of 'arrow1'.

-- An analysis of *P200 is a spear blade* which contains 'blade1' (part of an instrument) is preferred over one containing 'blade2' (loud jovial man), because the context activation of 'blade1' was higher than that of 'blade2'.

Text no. A14:

> Plexir manufactures P9999 which is a computer. It is supplied by Smith. P1010 is a terminal that is supplied by Clark. This one is made by Mikota. These machines are red.
>
> P9000 is a green printer. It is made by Plexir. P4444 is a blue computer. The cost of the machine is 7850. The peripheral is supplied by the P9999 supplier. The terminal manufacturer makes the blue machine. The cost of Mikota's peripheral is 235.

Examples:

-- The analyser produces two analyses for the sentence *P1010 is a terminal that is supplied by Clark*, one of which contains the sense 'terminal1' (a computer peripheral), and the other 'terminal2' (a place, as in hovercraft-terminal). The analysis containing 'terminal1' is selected because it had a higher context activation than 'terminal2'. Similarly, the analysis of *This one is made by Mikota* that contains 'make1' (which corresponds to manufacturing) is preferred over an analysis containing another sense of *make*.

-- Two analyses are produced for *P9000 is a green printer*. One of these contains the senses 'green2' and 'printer1', and can be paraphrased as *The color of the printing machine P9000 is green*. The other contains the senses 'green1' and 'printer2', a possible paraphrase being *P9000 is a novice at printing*. The analysis containing the first combination of senses is chosen because the activation sum for this combination was higher.

-- During the interpretation of *The terminal manufacturer makes the blue machine*, the analyser representation of the compound *terminal manufacturer* presents 'terminal1' (peripheral), and 'terminal2' (place), as alternative senses for the modifier. The higher context activation of 'terminal1' means that it is chosen before the compound noun interpretation proceeds.

(3) Selection of analyses by case structure disambiguation

Choosing between alternative analyses of a sentence which are different in structure but have the same word senses is performed using a score based in part on context activation. The score includes the sum of the context activations of entities which are specializations of the case relationships present in a particular structure. The score also includes a bias for specialized case relationships over unspecialized ones. Most of the examples of structural disambiguation which have been processed by the system depend on this bias towards most specialized relationships rather than context activation.

An example of a sentence for which the analyser produces more than one case structure is *P4740 is manufactured by P5050's manufacturer in London*. In one of these structures the prepositional phrase *in London* is attached to the verb by the case label 'location'. In the other analysis the prepositional phrase is attached to the noun *manufacturer* again using the label 'location'. The disambiguation operation works by deriving from each analysis structure a set of entities representing specializations of the case labels present in the structure. This set of entities will consist of 'manufacture/agent' 'manufacture/obj', and 'manufacture/loc', for the analysis in which the prepositional phrase is attached to the verb, and the set of entities derived from the other analysis consists of 'manufacture/agent', 'manufacture/obj' and 'location'. In the example given the bias towards more specialized entities leads to the choice of the structure with the prepositional phrase attached to the verb, because 'manufacture/loc' is more specialized than 'location'. However, in situations where all the case relations have been specialized, the choice of structure depends solely on the context activations of the memory entities to which the case labels were specialized.

Structural disambiguation using context activation alone was specifically tested with the following example. Prior memory assertions were created stating that a 'supply1' statement has the 'location' case specialized to 'supplies/loc' and that this case can be filled by a 'city'. The text given below was then processed.

> P9999 is a disc-drive that is supplied by Smith. This peripheral is manufactured by Mikota. He supplies P7777 which is a terminal. It

is manufactured in London by Plexir. Clark supplies P9000 which is manufactured by Marconi in Paris.

The context mechanism is used to choose between two alternative structures produced by the analyser for the final sentence in the paragraph. In one of the analyses the prepositional phrase *in Paris* is attached to the embedded clause and the specialized case entities derived from the sentence were 'manufacture/obj', 'manufacture/agent', 'manufacture/loc', 'supplies/obje', and 'supplies/agent'. In the other structure the prepositional phrase is attached to the main clause, and the specialized case entities were 'manufacture/obj', 'manufacture/agent', 'supplies/obje', 'supplies/loc', and 'supplies/agent'. The first analysis was chosen because of the higher context activation sum for the specialized case entities derived from it.

It has not been possible with the Capture implementation to do any very thorough tests on the application of context activation to relationship interpretation in creation-mode or to structural disambiguation. These uses of context activation have only been tested in a few cases, primarily because context dependent ambiguities seem to arise less frequently from these cases than from the other cases discussed. However, the examples do show that it is relatively straightforward to apply context information in the style already described to a wide range of problems *without* complicating the Capture control structure.

7
Performing database capture

In this chapter I will describe details of performing the database capture task and aspects of sentence interpretation, including the handling of various clause types, which are necessary for making Capture into a working system. Towards the end of the chapter, we will turn to the more general questions of the coverage of constructions, the evaluation of the mechanisms through Capture, and the applicability of the techniques used in Capture to other text processing tasks.

7.1. The target databases

The target databases used to illustrate the processing which can be performed by the system are relational databases. The choice of the relational model for this purpose was made because the model is well known and has a reasonably well defined and simple organizational structure. Attributing semantics to a relational database is not a well defined process, although there have been attempts to incorporate semantic specification into variations on the relational model (e.g. Borkin's Semantic Relation Model, Borkin 1980). The information in memory about a database can be regarded as providing a kind of "conceptual schema", or at least a partial semantic definition, for the database which is adequate for performing the database capture task for simple texts. (It may be possible to provide more rigorous semantics for relational databases via their memory descriptions and the semantics of memory assertions discussed in Chapter 2, but this was not attempted.)

If a different database model had been used, then the form of the database descriptions in memory would have had to be changed (to a lesser or greater extent depending on the kind of data model involved), and so would the taskspecific operations, described later, which make use of these. However, the language interpretation operations and the context mechanism used with these operations would not be affected by the choice of a different database model. Examples indicating how the semantics of a relation in a relational database are expressed in memory were given in Section 6.1. Further details of this are included in Section 7.3.

Two test databases, the "Machines Database", dealing with data processing machines, and the "Artifacts Database", about museum artifacts, were used. The "enterprise", in database systems jargon, for the (somewhat unrealistic) Machines Database could be a retail organization which wished to keep track of descriptions of the data processing machines (models) which it marketed, and their suppliers and manufacturers. In this database MACHINES/RELATION gives the model number, its cost, categorization into machine type (e.g. computer or printer), the weight of the model, and its color. The MANUFACTURES/RELATION specifies the model number, the manufacturer name, and the city of manufacture. The SUPPLIERS/RELATION gives the names of suppliers and their status (which can be interpreted as credit status, or an indication of reliability). The SUPPLIES/RELATION records the suppliers who supply particular models.

For the Artifacts Database the enterprise is envisaged to be an anthropology museum, the database being created from natural language records about artifacts and collectors. In this database ARTIFACTS/RELATION gives the number of an artifact, its condition, and a categorization of its type (e.g. ornament or weapon). The ORIGIN/RELATION specifies the collector of an artifact and its place of collection. The COLLECTORS/RELATION gives a collector's name, occupation (e.g. missionary), and nationality. The test databases thus have a modest level of complexity, and certainly cover data broad enough to challenge the interpretation mechanism if described in running text.

The specific column names of the relations in the two databases are listed below. Underlined columns indicate the attributes forming a key for each relation.

(A) Machines Database

MACHINES/RELATION

<u>MC/MCNUM</u> MC/COST MC/TYPE MC/COLOR MC/WEIGHT

SUPPLIERS/RELATION
S/SID S/STATUS
SUPPLIES/RELATION
SMC/SID SMC/MCNUM
MANUFACTURES/RELATION
M/MNAME M/MCNUM M/CITY

(B) Artifacts Database

ARTIFACTS/RELATION
ARTF/NUMB ARTF/TYPE ARTF/COND
ORIGIN/RELATION
ORIG/ARTN ORIG/COLL ORIG/PLAC
COLLECTORS/RELATION
COLL/NAME COLL/OCCP COLL/NATN

The keys specified above are the only candidate keys for the relations. The functional dependencies which are assumed to hold for the two enterprises can be summarized by saying that all the relations are in "third normal form". Thus there is no functional dependency between, say, the color of machines and their cost, or between the occupation and nationality of collectors (explanations of functional dependency and third normal form are given in many database system textbooks, such as Date (1981)).

One reason for handling two domains (and corresponding target databases) was to increase the range of example texts. A second reason was to verify that a change in the domain and target database would involve only additions to the contents of memory (unless it turned out in practice that the different domains naturally led to input texts of substantially different complexity). This limitation of changes to memory only does hold for Capture proper (i.e. excluding the analyser and its dictionary) as far as the tests went, although processing examples from a second domain did bring to light a number of "bugs" in the implementation.

7.2. Database management system assumptions

A number of assumptions were made about the capabilities of the database management system to which the information extracted from the texts would be passed, but care was taken to make these sensible ones, matching the current state of DBMS research (though they were perhaps in advance of current commercial DBMS). The first assumption is that the DBMS is thought of as operating under the "open world assumption". That is, assertions corresponding to tuples that are not included in relations are interpreted as being unknown, rather than false. This is because the database capture task being performed is thought of as a process of accumulating information rather than updating an existing complete model of the world described by the database.

A second and necessary assumption, related to the open world assumption, refers to the treatment of null values in the database. It is assumed that the DBMS allows "null" or unknown values for entries in non-key columns. For instance, a tuple in the 'MACHINES/RELATION' with key 'P9000' can have the 'MC/COLOR' entry unknown. This is a necessary assumption for many of the applications envisaged for database capture from text, because the texts used need not have been written with a particular data model in mind, and only known or observed information, which may not be complete, will be recorded in the texts. Further, it is not always possible to specify default values for particular columns of relations. A mechanism for default values is in any case often considered to be the responsibility of the DBMS. (Nevertheless the framework of the Capture system can, I believe, straightforwardly accommodate task-specific operations for some handling of default database values, which would be specified in the descriptions of database relations in memory.)

A third assumption is that the DBMS can enforce constraints about a particular database in such a way that some of the information passed to it by the text processing system could be ignored, or could lead to other side effects in the database such as the deletion of a tuple. As noted earlier, it is assumed that the DBMS has no way of communicating about these events to the text processing system and that therefore they cannot affect the interpretation of the text. Thus, for example, if the sentence *P9000 is green* is encountered, and then *P9000 is red*, it is for the DBMS to perform an update, or to ignore the information generated by the text processor for the second sentence because it is considered to violate a constraint.

In summary, the text processing system assumes that it is sending information to a sophisticated DBMS which has its own means for dealing with incomplete or even inconsistent information. The database descriptions represented in memory are thus not intended to help the DBMS carry out its functions, but only to allow the text processing system to generate information from text which may be used by a DBMS. The techniques used for describing databases in memory could perhaps be useful for a DBMS since such a description can be regarded as a high level conceptual schema. Similar techniques have indeed been tried for this purpose, but the problems involved are considered to be database theory problems (as yet largely unresolved), and only the text processing issues that are relevant to the database capture task have been considered in the present work.

One consequence of the assumptions just listed is that the interface between the text processing system and the DBMS is very simple. The output of the task specific processing component of Capture is a list of "database creation statements". Each database creation statement has the form

(relation-name ((column-name$_1$ value$_1$) ... (column-name$_n$ value$_n$))).

One, or more, of the column names in a creation statement must form the "key", or "joint key", for the relation in the statement. For example, processing the sentence *Plexir supplies P7720 which is a computer* results in the following two database creation statements

(SUPPLIES/RELATION ((SMC/SID Plexir) (SMC/MCNUM P7720)))
(MACHINES/RELATION ((MC/MCNUM P7720) (MC/TYPE computer))).

'MC/MCNUM' is the key for the 'MACHINES/RELATION', and 'SMC/SID' and 'SMC/MCNUM' form the key for the 'SUPPLIES/RELATION'.

A post-processor can translate database creation statements into a request in the data manipulation language (DML), for example SEQUEL (Chamberlin et al. 1976), of the DBMS to incorporate the new information into the target database. The post-processor would do this using a simple syntactic transformation. For the first database creation statement, a SEQUEL-like statement might be

```
INSERT INTO SUPPLIES/RELATION (SMC/SID, SMC/MCNUM):
  <Plexir, P7720>.
```

The assumption that the DBMS can handle unknown values is relevant here because it allows database creation statements which do not contain all column names to be translated into a DML statement for inserting a tuple into the database. As remarked by Gray (1981, p.148) "When there are unknown values in a database, it is not always appropriate to reject a request for the insertion of a new tuple whose key matches that of an existing tuple. It may be possible to merge the information in them." For the second database creation statement above, the SEQUEL-like statement might therefore be

```
INSERT INTO MACHINES/RELATION (MC/MCNUM, MC/TYPE):
  <P7720, computer>.
```

A further database creation statement generated from a later sentence might be

```
(MACHINES/RELATION ((MC/MCNUM P7720) (MC/COST 900)))
```

with the corresponding DML statement

```
INSERT INTO MACHINES/RELATION (MC/MCNUM, MC/COST):
  <P7720, 900>.
```

It is assumed that the DBMS would merge the information (i.e. cost is 900) from the second INSERT statement into the tuple created by the first one.

In a production system it would also be necessary to replace the word senses which currently appear in database creation statements with surface lexical stems, or with database specific codes (e.g. for colors). The information required for doing this can easily be represented in memory if necessary. The following section will describe how database creation statements are generated by the task-specific component of Capture. However, the material given is very specific to the application task, and the reader may wish to skip through many of the details appearing in the section.

7.3. Task-specific operations

The memory retrieval operations specific to the database capture task are concerned with locating those relational database description entities represented in memory which correspond to language related entities in memory. The retrieval operations know about the form in which these database descriptions are represented in memory. As explained in Section 6.1, a relational database is described in terms of collections of memory entities for each of the relations in it. These collections are structured by correspondence assertions (centered around an entity such as 'manufactures/relp') in order to encode the relationships between language related entities (e.g. 'manufacture'), predicates underlying relations (e.g. 'relp/manufactures') and database name entities (e.g. 'MANUFACTURES/RELATION'). Since the task-specific operations are implemented in terms of memory retrieval operations, they are ultimately executed in terms of the marker processing model.

Although clearly idiosyncratic to the database capture task, the task specific operations are not totally ad-hoc: they are independent of particular discourse domains and target databases. The operations can be classified into ones which either (a) locate entities describing the predicates underlying relations which correspond to linguistic entities, or (b) extract (and check) actual DBMS implementation names (i.e. the names of relations and columns) from among the entities describing the underlying predicates. Some of these operations are now described; the first three are of type (a), while the following three operations are of type (b).

(1) Locating underlying predicates

The predicates sought are specializations of language related and domain related predicate entities, 'manufacture' and 'color/of' for example. The operation simply finds a specialization of the language-derived predicate which is also asserted to be the 'relp/statement' of a relation (Section 6.1). For example, the following memory assertions

(Specialization: manufacture of make1)
(Specialization: relp/manufactures of manufacture)
(Corresponds: relp/manufactures to manufactures/relp as
relp/statement to db/relp)

are used to locate the underlying predicate entity 'relp/manufactures' from the language predicate entity 'make1'.

(2) Classification of database entities

In both the test databases one or more of the underlying predicates classified individual entities in the database domain. These classifications appear in the target databases as the columns for machine type, artifact type and collector occupation. The task-specific operation is given a memory entity, 'P997' say, which is an instance of a type of object in the database domain, and if possible returns an entity which is a valid classification of the object for that database. For example, the artifact type for 'P790', known to be an armlet, would be 'ornament1'. Similarly 'P9000', a minicomputer, would yield 'computer'. The memory assertions used for the first example are

(Specialization: P790 of armlet1 (instance))
(Specialization: P790 of artifact/dbentity)
(Specialization: armlet1 of ornament1)
(Corresponds: db/artifact/types to artifact/dbentity as
dbentity/classif to dbentity)
(Specialization: ornament1 of db/artifacts/types).

The last two memory assertions encode task-specific knowledge which asserts that 'ornament1' is a valid database classification in the Artifacts Database. In another database, for instance one about jewelry prices, the entity 'armlet1' might itself be a valid classification, though it is not in the Artifacts Database. The database classification operation finds the generic database entity, e.g. 'artifact/dbentity', for the object that it is given, and then uses the 'dbentity/classif' associated with this to choose an entity which is a valid classification and which is above the entity being classified in one of the hierarchies.

(3) Locating database entities

An operation of this type would, for instance, be given the domain-related entity 'armlet1' and return 'artifact/dbentity', and similarly 'disc-drive1' would return 'machine/dbentity'. The following memory assertions are used by the operation in the second example.

(Specialization: disc-drive1 of peripheral)
(Specialization: peripheral1 of machine)
(Specialization: machine/dbentity of machine)
(Corresponds: machine/dbentity to supplies/relp as
relp/dbentity to db/relp)

The entity returned by the operation fills the role of a 'relp/dbentity' in a database description and shares an ancestor, in the specialization hierarchy, with the domain-related entity given to the operation.

(4) Database names for predicate arguments

This operation locates the names, in the target database, of the column and relation appropriate to a database value, where this value has been asserted to be the argument of an instance of an underlying predicate for the relation. For example, suppose we are given these memory assertions:

(Specialization: E22 of relp/machine/weight (instance))
(Corresponds: 290 to E22 as
machine/weight/value to relp/machine/weight)

and have a part of the database description as follows

(Specialization: MACHINES/RELATION of relation (instance))
(Corresponds: MACHINES/RELATION to machine/relp as
relp/relation to db/relp)
(Specialization: MC/WEIGHT of column (instance))
(Corresponds: machine/weight/entry to machine/relp as
relp/entry to db/relp)
(Corresponds: machine/weight/value to machine/weight/entry as
relp/entry/value to relp/entry)
(Corresponds: MC/WEIGHT to machine/weight/entry as
relp/entry/column to relp/entry)
(Corresponds: relp/machine/weight to machine/relp as
relp/statement to db/relp)
(Corresponds: machine/weight/value to relp/machine/weight as
weight/of/weight to weight/of).

The relevant underlying predicate is the entity 'relp/machine/weight' and the relevant generic argument to it is 'machine/weight/value'. Retrieval operations for finding fillers of (inherited) roles in correspondence assertions make use of the assertions listed above to locate 'machine/weight/entry', and then the column name 'MC/WEIGHT'. The same types of retrieval operations make use of the correspondence assertions to locate the entity 'machine/relp', and from this the relation 'MACHINES/RELATION'.

In general, however, locating the correct relation and column names is not simply a matter of following a prescribed chain of role-owner relationships in correspondence assertions. Thus the 'relp/entry', with which the entities 'relp/entry/column' and 'relp/entry/value' are associated, may have its 'relp/entry/value' filled by the name, or number, of a database entity rather than by a simple value (such as the weight value above). For example, the other argument of the predicate instance 'E22' may have been filled by inclusion of the assertion

(Corresponds: P9999 to E22 as machine/dbentity to relp/weight/of)

where the following assertions, in addition to those given above, appear in the database description:

(Specialization: MC/MCNUM of column (instance))
(Corresponds: machine/mcnum/entry to machine/relp as
relp/entry to db/relp)
(Corresponds: mcnum/value to machine/mcnum/entry as
relp/entry/value to relp/entry)
(Corresponds: mcnum/value to machine/dbentity as
dbentity/number to numbered/dbentity)
(Corresponds: machine/dbentity to relp/machine/weight as
weight/of/possessor to weight/of)
(Specialization: machine/dbentity of numbered/dbentity).

To locate the column 'MC/MCNUM' the operation uses the entity 'mcnum/value' instead of the generic argument of the underlying predicate (i.e. 'machine/dbentity').

Thus the task-specific operation for locating column names from predicate arguments needs to check whether the predicate argument is described as a numbered or named database entity, and then to use an appropriate "role", 'dbentity/name' or 'dbentity/number', of the database entity to locate the column name in the database description.

Another complication in this operation is that the generic underlying predicate argument, for instance 'machine/dbentity' in the last example, may take part in the description of more than one relation. The appropriate names are selected using the context mechanism (see (7) below).

(5) Database names for classification

I have explained how a database entity, such as 'P790', because it is an 'armlet1' and an 'artifact/dbentity', can be given a classification, 'ornament1', with respect to a target database. The part of the database description which allows this to be done also indicates the database names which are used to encode this classification in the target database. Simple role extraction retrieval operations, specified by this task-specific operation, are used to obtain this information once the 'dbentity/classif' (see (2) above) for the database entity has been identified. For the armlet example this entity is 'db/artifact/types', the relation name is 'ARTIFACTS/RELATION', the column for 'P970' is 'ARTF/NUMB', and the column for 'ornament1' is 'ARTF/TYPE'. The relevant memory assertions, in addition to the ones given in (2), are as follows:

(Corresponds: db/artifact/types to artifact/dbentity as
dbentity/classif to dbentity)

(Corresponds: ARTIFACTS/RELATION to db/artifact/types as
classif/relation to dbentity/classif)
(Corresponds: ARTF/NUMB to db/artifact/types as
classif/id/col to dbentity/classif)
(Corresponds: ARTF/TYPE to db/artifact/types as
classif/type/col to dbentity/classif).

(6) Checking for keys

This operation simply checks that a list of entities representing columns includes all the columns in the key for a relation. For example, the operation succeeds if it is given the columns 'SMC/SID' and 'SMC/MCNUM', and the relation 'SUPPLIES/RELATION'. The relevant memory assertions in this case are

(Corresponds: SMC/MCNUM to SUPPLIES/RELATION as
rel/key/col to relation)
(Corresponds: SMC/SID to SUPPLIES/RELATION as
rel/key/col to relation).

(7) Context application for task-specific operations

(7a) Selecting database names. Context is not only applied to linguistic interpretation problems, it is also used in connection with the specific needs of the database capture component. The context activation of the entities forming descriptions of database relations allows the correct column names in the database implementation to be selected. The task-specific retrieval operation for selecting generic database entries (i.e. specializations of 'relp/entry', see (4) above) chooses among alternative entities on the basis of their context activation. In fact the context factors which allow the selection of the correct database-related entities are explicitly controlled by task-specific operations (they are created after the creation of an instance of an underlying predicate for that relation). Selecting database names is a local (clause level) application of context information. Explicit control is possible for task-specific operations because they are better defined, and hence easier to control, than language interpretation operations. An example of this application of context is

P9000 is supplied by Smith. The cost of the machine is 200.

The column name 'SMC/MCNUM' (the machine number column in the 'SUPPLIES/RELATION') is chosen during the processing of the first sentence whereas 'MC/MCNUM' (the machine column in the 'MACHINES/RELATION') is chosen for the second sentence.

A more interesting application of context for the database capture task is the selection between alternative underlying predicates.

(7b) Selecting database predicates. The implemented system allows context application for choosing between alternative underlying predicates ((1) above) on the basis of context activation. An example of a situation in which context was applied for this purpose is as follows. A column for the color of an artifact was added to the Artifacts Database; there is a color column already in the Machines Database. The underlying predicates referring to color in the descriptions in memory of the two databases were the entities 'relp/artifact/color' and 'relp/machine/color' respectively. A single "confusing" text was created to test the application of context to sorting out the appropriate underlying predicates. The text processed using this modified description of the Artifacts Database is given below.

> P500 is an armlet. It was collected by Haddon. P550 is red.
> P9000 is a disc-drive that is supplied by Smith. The cost of the machine is 200. P9900 is red.

The underlying predicate chosen during the processing of *P550 is red* was 'relp/artifact/color'. The other underlying predicate that was a specialization of 'color/of', 'relp/machine/color', was preferred during the interpretation of *P9900 is red.* These choices were made according to context activation; and as a result appropriate database creation statements were generated.

The operations described in this section provide the task-specific component of the Capture system with the necessary tools for exploiting the database-related knowledge represented in memory. The way these operations are used in performing the database capture task is explained in Section 7.5 below.

7.4. Sentence processing in Capture

As we discussed in Section 6.3, clause interpretation operations are procedures which embody the overall flow of control in the Capture system. They involve applying the memory and context mechanisms to solving interpretation problems, for instance reference resolution, which have already been described.

They also involve the evaluation of task-specific operations leading to the generation of database creation statements. Thus before discussing how the database capture task is carried out, we should examine clause interpretation and related operations.

(1) Sentence interpretation

"Interpret-sentence" is the highest level interpretation operation below the "interpret-paragraph" operation. This latter operation only alters context information (Section 6.2); for the present purpose it is sufficient to say that, interpret-paragraph having been applied, each of the sentences in the paragraph is interpreted using interpret-sentence.

The interpret-sentence operation performs two functions. The first of these is calling appropriate disambiguation operations for selecting between alternative structures produced by the analyser for the sentence if more than one analysis is produced. The second is calling the appropriate clause interpretation operations for the clauses in the selected analysis and handling the relationship between embedded and higher level clauses. Usually, when an embedded clause is encountered, interpret-sentence invokes the appropriate type of interpretation operation for this lower clause, and hands back a memory entity which is used by the operation interpreting the higher level clause. The memory entity which is passed back is the result of interpreting the noun phrase structure which is shared between the higher and lower clauses. This procedure is applied recursively to handle any depth of embedding.

An example is the interpretation of *Smith supplies the machine that is manufactured by Plexir*, for which the analysis structure is

```
(clause
 (type dcl)
 (tns present)
 (v (supply1 give
    (agent (n (Smith1 man)))
    (object
      ((trace (clause v object))
        (clause
          (type relative)
          (tns present)
          (aspect (passive))
          (v (manufacture make
```

```
(agent (n (Plexir1 *org)))
(object
  (n (machine thing (det (the1 one)))) ))) ))) ))).
```

The result of interpreting the shared structure (for *the machine*) would be a memory entity, such as 'P9999', so that the interpretation of the higher clause proceeds as though it were *Smith supplies P9999*. The procedure for handling embedded clauses is different for certain "be-clauses", e.g. *P9999 is a computer that is manufactured by Plexir*. For this example, the entity 'P9999' is passed down to the embedded clause, which is interpreted as though it were *P9999 is manufactured by Plexir.*

(2) Predicate clause interpretation

There are two predicate clause interpretation operations, which correspond to the two types of predicate clauses which are handled by the system. I will refer to the types of predicates, and the corresponding clauses, as "verbal" and "state" respectively. Each of the two clause interpretation operations leads to the construction of structures in memory which encode the propositional content of the clause. In both cases this involves the creation of a new predicate instance entity in memory.

The two operations will involve subsidiary operations for predicate and argument derivation. The interpretation of two different types of clauses, *be* and *have* clauses, is described in (4) below. Clauses that serve a referential function, such as restrictive relative clauses, are handled by reference resolution operations, and do not result in structure creation. The following description therefore applies only to the top level processing of the verbal and state types of clause.

(a) Verbal clause interpretation

Interpreting verbal clauses can be illustrated by the processing applied to the analyser's structure for *Plexir manufactures P777*, which is

```
(clause
  (type dcl)
  (tns present)
  (v (manufacture make
      (agent (n (Plexir1 *org)))
      (object (n (P777 thing)))) )).
```

The first step of processing is creating an instance of a predicate corresponding to the verb. The entity created is an instance of the entity corresponding to the verb sense (i.e. an instance of the entity 'manufacture'), or an instance of a specialization of the entity corresponding to the verb sense. The second alternative applies to the present example, the specialized predicate having been found by a task-specific operation. In both cases, by the associativity of specialization, the newly created entity, E1 say, is a specialization of the verb sense taken from the analyser clause representation.

Each case of the clause is now processed, usually in the order in which the filler of the case appears in the surface text (this order is recovered by the system, if possible, by comparing the output of the analyser with the original surface sentence). The case labels are specialized to the newly created predicate instance, E1 (see below). Thus 'agent' is specialized to 'supplier/dbentity' in this case, and the entity 'Plexir' is asserted to fill the 'supplier/dbentity' role for E1 by adding a correspondence assertion to memory. Similarly, 'P777' is asserted to correspond to the 'part/dbentity' of E1.

In the example 'Plexir' and 'P777' are explicit referents for which entities were assumed to exist in memory, and the subsidiary noun-arg interpretation operation which is given, for instance, the "noun-arg" (n (Plexir *org)), does not do any work. However, the situation appears the same from the point of view of the clause interpretation operation when the filler is more complex. Thus for the other types of noun-arg fillers a noun-arg interpretation operation is evaluated, parameterized by information such as the specialized role that the noun-arg fills, returning a unique memory entity which the clause interpretation operation can use as a filler. This is done for definite noun phrases, pronouns, and noun phrases referring to newly mentioned entities and sets of entities. The interpretation of embedded clauses also results in a memory entity so that the processing can continue as in the simple case.

(b) State clause interpretation

The parser produces state clause structures after analyzing adjectival phrases and *be* phrases predicating properties (as opposed to existence). The analyser structures constructed for these cases are the same. For example, the structure given below is constructed both for *P777 is red* and *The color of P777 is red* (and also for *the red P777* in a sentence containing this noun phrase).

```
(clause
  (type dcl)
  (tns present)
  (v (be2 be
     (agent (n (P777 thing)))
     (state (st (n (color NIL)) (val (red1 kind)))) ))).
```

The processing of anaphora and embedded clauses is handled in a manner which is transparent to the clause interpretation operation, in the style described for verbal clause interpretation above. So in order to explain the state-clause interpretation operation only a simple example is needed, say *P777 is red.* The first step of the operation is to create a predicate instance entity, E2 say, in memory. This entity is derived from the "state-arg"

(st (n (color NIL)) (val (red1 kind)))

which fills the state case of the clause, using a predicate specialization operation. The value of the state is also taken from the state-arg and is asserted to fill the specialization of the role 'be/state/value' for E2. In the context of the Machines Database the specialization for the example is 'machine/color/value' and the assertion

(Corresponds: red1 to E2 as machine/color/value to relp/machine/color)

is created in memory.

Similarly, the filler of the 'agent' case for the clause is asserted to fill the specialization of the role 'be/state/agent' for 'E2', and the following assertion is created

(Corresponds: P777 to E2 as machine/dbentity to relp/machine/color).

(3) Predicate and argument derivation

In the description of predicate clause interpretation above, I stated that predicates are derived during the interpretation of verb and state clause structures. In fact, the predicate entities in memory which correspond to the predicates for these clauses can be specialized by a task-specific operation, as is the case when the system is working in the database capture mode. This happens in a way which is transparent to the interpretation component, so that different task-specific components could return different predicate specializations, or a "null" task could simply always return the predicate entity unspecialized. However, ignoring this, locating generic predicate entities for these clause types is straightforward. Thus for verb clauses, the required predicate entity has the same name, e.g. supply1, as the verb sense in the clause, and the derivation of the predicate entity is immediate. The generic predicate entity for a state-clause is derived from the "state-arg" which fills the "state" case of the clause. Thus the state-arg for *These machines are blue* is

(st (n (color NIL)) (val (blue1 kind)))

and the corresponding generic predicate entity is 'color/of'. 'color/of' is found by evaluating a memory retrieval operation which searches for a specialization of 'be/state' that has 'color' filling its 'be/state/generic' role. The case labels in the analyser structures for the clauses must be specialized, if possible, to the arguments of the predicate entities, or to task specializations of these entities.

In both state and verb clauses, a memory retrieval operation, which can be described as "role-specialization", is used. This specializes role entities in memory to the most specific entities corresponding to them, i.e. the specialized arguments which are owned by the corresponding predicates. This depends on an assumption which Charniak calls the case-slot identity theory (Charniak 1981). This amounts to saying that the cases which can be identified from a linguistic analysis of a sentence can be identified with generic slots in a conceptual memory organized around frames.

The names of the generic role entities are derived from the case labels of the analyser dependency structures. For the verb cases of verb clauses the generic role entities have the same names as the case labels. For state clauses the case label 'agent' is mapped onto the role entity 'be/state/agent' and the case label 'value' is mapped onto 'be/state/value'. The generic (i.e. less specialized) role entities, though less informative, can still be used to continue processing when they cannot be refined by the role specialization operation.

As examples of specialized argument derivation, the case label "agent" in the analyser representation for *Plexir manufactures the machine* is mapped onto the entity 'agent' which is specialized, via 'make1/agent', to 'manufacture/agent', and the same label "agent" in the representation for *This artifact is fragile* is mapped onto the entity 'be/state/agent' and then specialized to the entity 'condition/of/possessor'.

(4) Be- and have-clause interpretation

The interpretation operations used for handling two special types of clauses, "be-clauses" and "have-clauses", are different in type from the predicate clause interpretation operations described earlier because the clauses are mapped directly into memory assertions, rather than memory entities representing a predicate instance. This is a consequence of the way memory is structured, i.e. specialization and correspondence assertions are closely connected with the classification and relationship senses of *be* and *have* respectively.

(a) Be-clause interpretation

This operation handles clauses like *P333 is a computer*, in which *is* asserts that an object can be described as fitting a certain type, i.e. generic concept. This sense of the verb *be* is output as "be1" by the analyser, instead of "be2", which is used for state assertions (these senses reflect the use of nominal and adjectival subject complements respectively). The structure for *P333 is a computer* output by the analyser is given below.

```
(clause
 (type dcl)
 (tns present)
 (v
  (be1 be
   (agent
    (n (P333 thing)))
   (object
    (n (computer thing (det (a1 one)))) )))).
```

The memory assertion created by be-clause interpretation is a specialization assertion. The operation involves finding, or creating, the entities for the arguments of the specialization assertion corresponding to the be-clause and then adding this assertion to memory. This is straightforward for the example clause, and the new memory assertion is

(Specialization: P333 of computer (instance)).

The specific entity, 'P333', is taken from the 'agent' case of the clause, and the generic entity, 'computer' in this example, is derived from the 'object' case. If there is no entity 'P333' in memory, a new entity is created.

More complex examples require further processing in order to determine the generic and specific entities. Examples are

(1) This machine is a computer.

(2) Wintron is a computer manufacturer.

(3) P7780 is a disc-drive that is made by Plexir.

In (1) the noun phrase *this machine* is handled by reference resolution and an entity is returned and used, in the same way as for definite references in verb-clause and state-clause interpretation. In (2) the compound *computer manufacturer* is analyzed by compound noun interpretation in what was called "creation mode". The compound noun interpretation creates, or locates, a memory entity that corresponds to *computer manufacturer*, E17 say, and the new memory assertion for the clause is

(Specialization: Wintron of E17 (instance)).

For sentence (3) the interpretation of the main clause is straightforward, but the embedded structure (for *disc-drive made by Plexir*) cannot be handled in the normal way because this would lose the information that the referent of *disc-drive* in this clause is known to be 'P7780'. Thus before the embedded clause is handled by evaluating a verb-clause interpretation operation, 'P7780' is attached to the noun-arg structure for *disc-drive*, so precluding normal definite reference resolution, and the embedded structure is then interpreted as *P7780 is made by Plexir*.

(b) Have-clause interpretation

As with be-clause interpretation, the interpretation of have-clauses leads to the creation of memory assertions, to represent their propositional content, which in this case are correspondence assertions. An example is the clause *it has a bolt*, for which the analysis structure is

```
(clause
  (type dcl)
  (tns present)
  (v
    (have8 have
      (agent
        (n (it dummy)))
      (object
        (n (bolt1 thing (det (a1 one)))) )))) ).
```

The correspondence assertion which is created for this would be (assuming 'P9980' is the referent for *it*)

(Corresponds: E18 to P9980 as machine/component to machine).

Here E18 is a newly created entity which is asserted to be a specialization of 'bolt1'. A pair of entities is derived from the 'agent' and 'object' cases of the clause. A memory operation for finding the relationship between this pair of memory entities is evaluated in order to find as specific a relationship as possible that can be used in the correspondence assertion. Thus this interpretation operation tries to make the relationship described by the have-clause more explicit before its propositional content is incorporated in memory. Again, this interpretation operation can lead to the evaluation of reference and compound noun operations. An example of this is *The machine supplied by Smith has an adjustment bolt.*

7.5. Interleaving interpretation and task operations

We should now consider at what point the task processor evaluates task-specific memory operations so that it can produce the database creation statements corresponding to the text. In fact the evaluation of task-specific and language interpretation operations is interleaved in a simple manner. An alternative to this mode of processing would be to perform the necessary interpretation operations on all of the output of the analyser for the text before evaluating the task-specific operations required to produce the database creation statements. But this is a less satisfactory control regime.

Thus there are two reasons why interpretation and task operations should be interleaved. First, interleaving allows the interpretation process to make use of certain assumptions about entities in the database domain. For example, the interpretation process might be able to make use of the assumption that in the database world the 'object' case of manufacturing actions is normally filled by a 'machine'. The intention is to be able to make use of such a restriction without its persisting when the database specific part of memory is removed. An example of how this works is given later in this section. The second reason for interleaving has to do with accumulating context information. The evaluation of task-specific operations leads to the creation of context factors. This can, in principle, aid subsequent interpretation operations if, for example, the context activations of entities concerned with the database domain are increased directly as a result of the creation of these context factors, or indirectly if association or subject area context factors are created.

The sequences of task-specific operations which are evaluated for handling predicate clauses (verb and state clauses) are different from those for handling be-clauses.

Predicate clauses

After the generic predicate entity for the clause, e.g. 'manufacture' or 'weight/of', has been identified, a task-specific operation for specializing this predicate entity is evaluated. In the database capture task this is the operation to which we referred as locating underlying predicates (Section 7.3(1)), and it would return 'relp/manufactures' for 'manufacture' and 'relp/machine/weight' for 'weight/of'. The predicate instance entity created for the clause is asserted to be a specialization of the underlying predicate. The evaluation of the task-specific operation has now been completed and control is returned to the clause interpretation operation, which need not know whether the predicate instance was in fact specialized to an underlying predicate for a relation.

However, if the newly created predicate instance has been asserted to be an underlying predicate, this can affect the evaluation of argument specialization and reference resolution operations which are initiated by the clause interpretation operation. For example, during the interpretation of the sentence *It is manufactured by Plexir*, the predicate entity 'manufacture' is specialized to 'relp/manufactures' so that the argument entity derived from the case label 'object' is not 'manufacture/obj' but 'machine/dbentity'. The fact that the object case may be described as a 'machine/dbentity' can be used as a constraint by the reference resolution operation which is evaluated for the pronoun *it*.

The clause interpretation operation evaluates reference resolution operations for each of the noun phrases of the clause, the referents in the current example being 'Plexir1' and a particular 'machine/dbentity', 'P9000' say. Control then reverts to the task processor. This evaluates a task-specific operation for finding the database relation and column names for each of the arguments of the instance of the underlying predicate created for the clause. The task processor then merges the information which results from evaluating these task-specific operations into one or more database creation statements.

For instance, the following database creation statement is output for *It is manufactured by Plexir*:

(MANUFACTURES/RELATION ((M/MCNUM P9000) (M/MNAME Plexir1))).

An example in which the underlying predicate is derived from a state-clause is *The weight of the machine is 220*. The interleaving of interpretation and task-specific operations is the same as for the verb-clause case, so the database creation statement output by the task processor might be

(MACHINES/RELATION ((MC/MCNUM P8000) (MC/WEIGHT 220))).

Finally, an operation is evaluated to check that the set of column names in the database creation statement(s) includes the columns in the key of the target relation as specified in memory.

Be-clauses with nominal complements

The output produced by the task processor for the sentence *P2000 is an armlet* is

(ARTIFACTS/RELATION ((ARTF/NUMB P2000) (ARTF/TYPE ornament1))).

A be-clause interpretation operation begins processing the analyser representation of the clause by identifying, or creating, the generic entity for the clause, which is simply 'armlet1' in this case. It also evaluates a reference resolution operation for identifying, or creating, the referent of the subject of the clause (i.e. the entity whose description is being refined by the clause) which in this case is the entity 'P2000'. 'P2000' is then asserted to be a specialization of 'armlet1'. At this point the be-clause interpretation operation activates the task processor which handles the consequences, for the task, of the new specialization assertion.

The task processor evaluates an operation to find a generic database entity for the entity 'P2000'. This operation returns 'artifact/dbentity', and the following assertion is included in memory:

(Specialization: P2000 of artifact/dbentity).

The task processor then evaluates an operation to find a classification of 'P2000' with respect to the Artifacts Database. This operation succeeds for 'P2000', and 'ornament1' is returned as a valid classification. Since the classification operation has succeeded, the task processor evaluates an operation which enables it to construct the database creation statement given above by extracting the relation and column names from the description of the Artifacts Database.

Embedded clauses

The task-specific processing for an embedded clause occurs (in the manner described above for predicate-clauses and be-clauses) at the time at which the embedded clause is interpreted, i.e. before the interpretation of the higher level clause has been completed. Thus the task output for embedded clauses is produced first; for example, the output produced for the sentence *Plexir manufactures P9000 which is supplied by Smith* is

(SUPPLIES/RELATION ((SMC/SID Smith1) (SMC/MCNUM P9000)))
(MANUFACTURES/RELATION ((M/MNAME Plexir1) (M/MCNUM P9000))).

Similarly, the sentence *P9000 is a computer that is manufactured by Mikota* results in the following database creation statements

(MANUFACTURES/RELATION ((M/MNAME Mikota1) (M/MCNUM P9000)))
(MACHINES/RELATION ((MC/TYPE computer) (MC/MCNUM P9000))).

Some embedded clauses do not convey new information, and these do not generate any database creation statements. Restrictive relative clauses, which are interpreted by reference resolution operations, are of this type. For instance the sentence *Plexir manufactures the computer that is supplied by Smith*, might produce the output

(MANUFACTURES/RELATION ((M/MNAME Plexir1) (M/MCNUM P9000)))

Verb and state clauses for which the clause predicates cannot be specialized to the underlying predicate for a relation in the target database do not generate any database creation statements. An example of such a clause is *Haddon donated P1234*. Nonetheless, the memory interpretation of such clauses is still important for the database capture task because the information conveyed by them might be necessary for later processing, for instance reference resolution in the interpretation of the sentence *The artifact that was donated by Haddon comes from Woodlark.*

Plurals

The task processing for clauses with plural noun phrases can result in the generation of more than one database creation statement. The memory interpretation of such clauses involves retrieving, or creating, a memory entity that represents the set of objects referred to by the plural noun phrase. For example during the interpretation of the sentence *Smith supplies P9000 and P9090* an entity, 'E1' say, will have been created, and also the following assertions

> (Specialization: P9000 of E1 (member))
> (Specialization: P9090 of E1 (member))
> (Corresponds: E1 to E2 as machine/dbentity to relp/supplies).

The task-specific operations initiated by the task processor will return 'E1' and 'Smith' as well as the database names. This is because it is 'E1' which fills the 'machine/dbentity' argument of the underlying predicate instance 'E2'. The task processor evaluates a retrieval operation for locating the elements of the set represented by 'E1' and then produces the following database creation statement

> (SUPPLIES/RELATION ((SMC/SID Smith1) (SMC/MCNUM P9090)))
> (SUPPLIES/RELATION ((SMC/SID Smith1) (SMC/MCNUM P9000))).

Similarly, the output generated for the sentence *They supply the printers* might be

> (SUPPLIES/RELATION ((SMC/SID Smith1) (SMC/MCNUM P1000)))
> (SUPPLIES/RELATION ((SMC/SID Smith1) (SMC/MCNUM P2000)))
> (SUPPLIES/RELATION ((SMC/SID Clark1) (SMC/MCNUM P1000)))
> (SUPPLIES/RELATION ((SMC/SID Clark1) (SMC/MCNUM P2000))).

7.6. Handling other constructions

However, there are different categories of construction which cannot be handled by the Capture system, so database creation statements are not generated for them. Some of these represent genuine limitations to the system. The main categories of excluded constructions are

(1) Constructions which cannot be handled by the analyser or by the interpretation component.

(2) Constructions which cannot be mapped into database creation statements because of the rather restricted data modeling capabilities of relational databases.

(3) Cases for which the mapping into database creation statements depends on inference mechanisms not supplied in the Capture project.

(4) Cases which could be handled if the task-specific operations were more sophisticated.

(5) Constructions which could be handled if additional task-specific operations were defined.

Examples of categories (1), (2), and (3) will be given below under the heading "limitations" and examples of (4) and (5) under the heading "extensions". Needless to say, these examples represent only a sample and there are many other constructions that would not be handled by the system.

Limitations on coverage

(1a) Problems due to the incomplete coverage of grammatical constructions by the analyser. In this group we have sentences with conjunctions (except for simple noun phrase conjunctions); certain types of elliptical sentences; and sentences in which relationships exhibit parallelism with surface word order. Examples are

Plexir manufactures and supplies P2000
So does Mikota
Clark and Nilfisk traveled to Daui in that order
P200 and P700 were collected by Clark and Nilfisk respectively.

(1b) Problems arising from deficiencies in the interpretation mechanisms. These include coping with negation, metaphor, and idioms. Examples are

The condition of P900 is not good
The spear head is razor sharp
Haddon tried to pull the wool over their eyes.

(2a) Comparatives cause problems for database input. The first example below would require allowing the use of ranges of values in the database.

P700 is older than P900
The condition of P700 is better than the condition of P200

(2b) Uncertain facts expressed with modals. For example *This artifact might have been collected in Daui.*

(2c) A type of quantification that cannot be handled by the database capture task is exemplified by *Two of them are from Woodlark.*

(3a) The database capture component always assumes a distributive interpretation of statements such as *The cost of the machines is 200.* Even though the interpretation component does not commit itself to choosing a distributive or collective interpretation, translation into database creation statements must do this.

(3b) Cases which require rule-based reasoning to manipulate structures created by the interpretation component. In order to deal with these a mechanism for applying rules represented in memory would have to be implemented (cf. the mapping rules in Consul, Mark 1981). Examples are *P700 arrived with P200* (implying that they were collected at the same place); *P300 was bought from a Woodlark trader* (possibly implying that the origin of the artifact is Woodlark); and *P400 should be handled with care* (implying that the artifact should be classified as fragile).

Extensions of coverage

(4a) The database descriptions could include a specification of allowable state value descriptions so that *The condition of this artifact is excellent* would lead to 'good' via the relationship in memory between the entities 'good' and 'excellent'. A similar extension is possible for place names and would make use of knowledge of spatial inclusion for regions.

(4b) Examples like *Bevan supplied us with a canoe-prow from Daui* show that the operation identifying underlying database predicates should check the restrictions on the arguments of the underlying predicates. In the Capture implementation these restrictions were only used to aid the interpretation process.

(5a) There are a number of constructions for which specialization assertions should be created in a way similar to their creation during the interpretation of be-clauses. Examples are

> P300 is a fine example of shell currency
> These artifacts were used as currency in the Massim area.

(5b) A variant on the above is those compound noun phrases which should be handled in a similar way to be-clauses when the compound introduces a new object as well as conveying information about it. An example is *the canoe paddle P790* in sentences like

The canoe paddle P790 was collected by Nilfisk.

(5c) Relationship interpretation affects the generation of database creation statements indirectly, via reference resolution. An additional task-specific operation could be implemented in order to generate database creation statements on the basis of relationship interpretation. For example, if there was a relation in the Artifacts Database listing the parts of artifacts, then a suitable database creation statement would be generated after interpreting the relationship in *The pot has a lid.*

(5d) For the purpose of generating database creation statements, a task-specific operation could be defined which would allow the inheritance of specified properties from roles to owners in correspondence assertions. For example, given the sentence *The pot's lid is in poor condition* we may wish to state in the database that the condition of the whole assembly, pot plus lid, is poor.

(5e) Another necessary extension for a more complete system is the implementation of a task-specific operation for taking predicate names as values for specified database columns. For example, the Artifacts Database might have had a column indicating how an artifact was acquired by the museum. The values generated would then include "bought" and "bequeathed".

7.7. Evaluation of the mechanisms with Capture

Overall, the use of the techniques in the implemented Capture system was a success in that a number of simple texts were correctly processed, demonstrating non-trivial language interpretation and application task processing. This involved the use of a memory knowledge base consisting of around 450 entities and over 750 memory assertions, and the use of an interesting range of context factor types.

Thirty or so different short example texts were successfully processed by the system (as well as a similar number of non-interesting variants on these). The example texts in Appendix A (which includes the final output generated by these examples) pretty much exhaust the kinds of possibilities that the final version of the Capture system could handle with respect to the two target databases. It should be noted that exactly the same version of the Capture system (i.e. with the same initial contents of memory, and initial significance weights for context factor types, etc.) was used to produce all the output in Appendix A.

The implementation of the interpretation component concentrated on operations for solving common language interpretation problems. These operations seem to work reasonably robustly for the kind of simple descriptive texts which were processed by the system. In particular, memory is used during the interpretation of implicit relationships and various types of clauses, and the context mechanism is vital for the operations implemented for definite reference resolution, including plural references, and for word sense disambiguation (of the type which cannot be handled by the analyser).

The implementation of the database capture component illustrated the use of knowledge specific to an application task, including the relationships in memory between this knowledge and the language and domain related knowledge. The task required solutions to text interpretation problems such as reference resolution so that explicit database creation statements could be generated, and also knowledge of the domain so that, for example, entities could be classified with respect to the target database.

The size of the memory knowledge base used by the implemented system was probably too small for serious investigation of the advantages of using the indexing scheme, and clustering criteria used for indexing; for this, observation of the behavior of the system with a very large knowledge base, most of which would be irrelevant to any particular short text, would be necessary. Nevertheless, since the efficiency of memory processing (let alone access to the focus set) has been considered important enough for hardware designs to be investigated, investigations of the possibilities offered by software methods, such as those discussed in Chapter 8 below, are surely worthwhile.

Unfortunately, many of the artificial examples processed by Capture read somewhat awkwardly. This is partly due to the limitations on coverage at both the analysis and interpretation levels. Another reason is that devising texts for testing particular constructions meant that the most natural choice of linguistic expression to maintain cohesion was often sacrificed. Thus in some cases where pronouns would have been appropriate other types of definite reference were used instead (so it is just as well that this distinction was not being used to generate context information, as it probably should be in a more complete system). The management of context factors by different components was not fully tested in the implemented system. For example, the dependence on an existing parser meant that contributions of surface analysis to context were handled indirectly by the interpretation component rather than directly by the parser.

However, the mechanisms do provide a framework for carrying out more linguistically motivated investigations than were attempted here, e.g. studies of the interaction of factors contributed by different components to context, the relative importance of different factor types, and the extent to which this varies with different sorts of texts. There is the possibility of developing a successful theory for tricky problems in reference resolution, such as plural references and references to generics. The resolution of plural references is certainly a problem in which memory and context interact in a non-trivial way. Various possible algorithms could be devised which make use of memory and context in order to determine, for example, whether an existing set, a new set of entities, or a generic description is intended as the referent. The testing of various algorithms for reference and of theories about the interactions of context factors really needs to be done with respect to some corpus of collected texts.

The implemented system for database capture is still a long way from being an ideal production text processing system. Building such a system awaits solutions to a number of problems which are presently only poorly understood such as the processing of metaphors and robust parsing. Even a more modest system would require a large amount of work, using the techniques adopted in the implementation of Capture, for extending the coverage of the system as much as possible (see Section 3.5 and Section 7.6). However, the design of the Capture system could serve as the basis for practical semi-automated systems for database creation from collections of texts. A system of this kind would depend on the intervention of a human operator for resolving difficulties which it could not handle, and in this way would be similar to some proposed designs (see e.g. Kay 1980) for translation aids. The approach of finding simple solutions to common language interpretation problems taken in the design of Capture should make it a good starting point for building such a system. The quantifiable nature of context activation may also turn out to be an advantage. Decisions made by the system on the basis of context activation could be regarded as safe or not with respect to specified safety margins. For example, if the difference between the context activations of the best candidates for resolving a reference was less than such a margin then the human operator could be asked to confirm the decision taken by the system.

7.8. Applicability to similar tasks

As the discussion of restrictions on texts handled for database capture suggests, there are some restrictions on the other types of text processing application task which might be undertaken using the techniques explored in this project. For example only texts with limited domains of discourse can be handled, because we do not know, and are unlikely to know in the near future, how to represent in memory *all* of the knowledge required for text processing without a domain limitation. An example of a task requiring this knowledge might be summarizing all the articles in a news magazine. However, it has to be accepted that this is not a limitation specific to the Capture techniques. It applies to all knowledge-based approaches to language processing investigated to date. Another restriction is that the interpretation of the texts for the purpose of the task cannot depend on a deep understanding of human social affairs and goals (see e.g. Lehnert et al. 1983). This rules out such tasks as answering questions about the motivation of characters after reading passages from a novel. Research in this area is still at a very preliminary stage, and so there is not much to take over for inclusion in a Capture-like framework with wider applicability. Related to this restriction is another one also concerned with the representation of users' plans and goals. This is needed for sophisticated processing of texts conveying, for example, a sequence of instructions to be carried out by an automated office assistant. Another restriction is that the mechanisms techniques in the project do not cover the type of inference required for detailed analysis of causality and enablement for physical events (see e.g. Waltz 1981).

These restrictions would still permit a number of application tasks to be considered. One is gathering statistics from collections of natural language reports, such as medical reports (see Sager 1981), weather reports and financial market reports. Another possible application task is checking for the mention of specific facts or events when analyzing historical records. A related application is intelligent retrieval from collections of legal documents such as patent records (see e.g. Lebowitz 1983) or case reports. Another task associated with information retrieval is the automatic classification of documents by processing their abstracts. It seems plausible that the Capture techniques could be effectively applied to such types of task, and would improve on the use of more superficial automatic analysis techniques (for instance those described by King (1979) for historical records).

Given a well developed system based on the techniques used by Capture, the alterations to the system necessary for tailoring it to one of the above applications are as follows. It would be necessary to extend the dictionary to enable the analyser to parse sentences in the new domain. The design of the analyser as a general semantic parser (Boguraev and Sparck Jones 1983) means that, in principle, the changes to the dictionary would only involve the inclusion of new words and the addition of new word senses to existing entries. It would then be necessary to create memory entities for the new word senses and to relate them, using memory assertions, to existing entities in memory.

The above alterations would still be task independent. Further memory entities and assertions might have to be included in order to represent further restrictions and specializations applicable in the context of the task. Additional entities and assertions would also need to be included to represent knowledge specific to the application task itself. Finally it would be necessary to implement a task-specific component which would be invoked after the creation of memory assertions, or (roughly in the manner used in this project) at specific points during the processing of clauses, by the language interpretation component. The complexity of the task component and its task-specific memory operations would be very much a function of the complexity of the application task.

8

Techniques for efficient retrieval

The memory and context mechanisms depend on searches for entities that are marked with specified combinations of markers and also searches that are restricted by context activation thresholds. I would now like to discuss some indexing techniques aimed at efficient implementation of retrieval requests, and in particular the techniques used in Capture for indexing marked sets.

Although the techniques are aimed at reducing the amount of low level processing, on a serial machine, required for implementing the memory and context mechanisms, they are, for the most part, independent of the details of the representational formalism (and the actual operations which are performed) in that they are likely to apply to any system which makes use of the style of marker processing which has been described. More specifically, the techniques apply to the following.

(1) Intersection searches. Searching for sets of entities specified by marking conditions.

(2) Threshold searches. Searching for sets of entities whose activations are higher than a specified threshold.

(3) The effort involved in performing marker propagations.

The use of the techniques is purely motivated by efficiency since they do not affect the outcome of retrieval operations, and hence the outcome of interpretation operations which use the retrieval operations. However, the techniques, and the suggested extensions to them which were not implemented in Capture, are not merely low level implementation details: they address efficiency questions which are important for the realization of text processing systems exploiting "large" knowledge bases.

8.1. The indexing scheme and basic searches

Enhancing the efficiency of memory searches (i.e. (1) and (2) above) depends on indexing marked sets. For the purpose of this indexing a tree is constructed; the nodes representing memory entities are the leaves of this tree. The tree is constructed before any memory processing is performed, as follows. The nodes are partitioned into clusters of a chosen fixed size; the criteria for determining the order in which the nodes are put into clusters will be discussed later. (In the figure below each cluster has three nodes.) The nodes in each cluster are then linked to a newly created cluster-node with special clustering links. The cluster-nodes are then themselves clustered, and this is repeated until only one new cluster is created. This becomes the "indexing root", i.e. the root of the indexing tree formed by this procedure.

Marked sets are indexed during memory processing by marking nodes in the indexing tree. When any network node is marked, by a particular marker, all the cluster nodes above it are also marked by the same marker. (There are exceptions to this procedure which will be explained shortly.)

Searching for all network nodes with a given combination of markers (i.e. the set of nodes each of which is marked with all the markers in some specified set of markers) can be done by starting at the indexing root and following the combination down through those cluster nodes possessing it to the final selected network nodes. Similarly, searching for the nodes with activations that are higher than a specified threshold is performed by starting at the indexing root and only passing through cluster-nodes whose activations exceed the specified threshold. It should be noted that the markers attached to a cluster node and its corresponding activation do not play any semantic role since the cluster-nodes are only relevant to the indexing scheme.

The two types of search can be combined so that the cluster tree can be used to find the nodes with a given combination of markers that satisfy a threshold condition. Again, this search starts at the indexing root and only passes through cluster-nodes after it has been checked that their markers and activations satisfy the specified conditions.

An example search is for entities marked with "x" and "o" which have activation values greater than 100. Figure 8.1 shows an indexing tree in which the markers for memory entities (entities being the network nodes, i.e. the leaves of the tree) have been propagated up the tree in the manner described above. The significance weights for the markers are assumed to be those shown at the top right corner of the figure. For the marking configuration shown, there is only one memory entity satisfying the search condition. The nodes on the path indicated all "satisfy" the condition so the desired memory entity can be located by following this path.

Thus in order to reach target nodes for the types of searches which have been described we will only examine the network nodes in clusters for which the cluster-node satisfies the condition determining the target set. For the intersection search (i.e. searching with respect to a marker combination), these nodes are the network nodes in clusters that have a node marked with each of the markers in the combination. This means, in particular, that the number of network nodes examined will be bounded above by the cluster size times the number of nodes in the smallest marked set. On the other hand if the target set happens to be a union of the sets of nodes in clusters then only the network

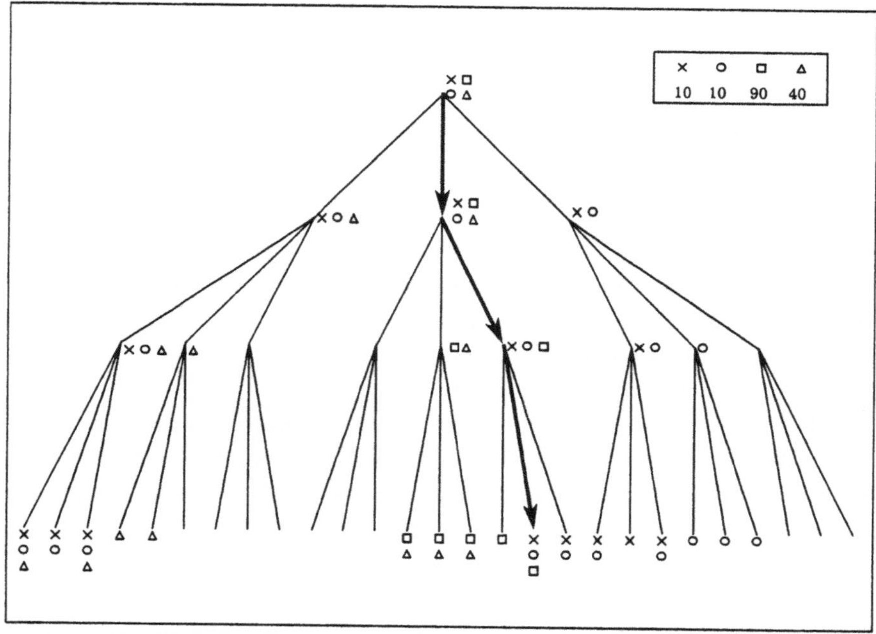

Figure 8.1. Example of a path from the root of the indexing tree

nodes in the intersection will be examined. A more detailed analysis of the simple intersection search, refining the bounds just given, is presented in Section 8.4 below.

Recorded propagations

The implementation of marker processing in the Capture system is complicated further by the use of "recorded propagations", which is also motivated by efficiency considerations. Recorded propagations are aimed at reducing the effort required for marking, as distinct from the effort required for searching addressed so far. In particular we would like to reduce the effort involved in repeating propagations which mark large sets of entities. A record is therefore kept of marker propagations that start from a single node and are expected to mark a large number of nodes. All the recorded propagations are marking operations of type (a) in the classification given in Section 2.3.

The record of the propagation is kept at the node at which the propagation starts. When a subsequent request is made for performing the same propagation the marker symbol noted in the record is returned, without generating a new marker symbol or marking any nodes.

Recording propagations in this way requires that these propagations be "maintained" when new assertions are added to memory. This is done by extending the propagations across links created for new assertions and marking nodes as appropriate. For example, assume that a propagation is recorded which marks all specializations of entity A, and that this propagation has marked entity B with a marker M. A new memory assertion (Specialization: C of B) will cause the propagation to be extended from B to C, and C will be marked with M. Extending propagations in this way during memory processing ensures that their markers can still be used validly in later processing. The fact that propagations can be recorded, and the way in which the representation of context depends on marked sets, means that the presence of a mark on a node can affect several memory operations, not just one.

Indexing negative conditions

As stated so far the scheme does not allow the inclusion in the search specification of conditions excluding nodes which are marked by any of the markers in a specified combination, or threshold searches when negative weights have been assigned to some markers. The necessary extension for dealing with this is now described.

The markers used to mark cluster nodes in the scheme described so far can be called "or-markers" in that they are used to mark a cluster node if *any* of the nodes below it are marked with the marker being indexed (or with the indexing marker - these were not distinguished in the above description). We can instead use an "and-marker" to mark a cluster node if *all* the nodes below it are marked with a particular marker (or the and-marker itself). If a marker is known to take part only in searches which specify that results should not be marked with it, we can index this marker with and-markers instead of or-markers. Then when a search involves this marker, cluster nodes which are marked with its indexing and-markers must not be passed through during the search, because it is known that they will not lead to any target network nodes.

And-markers can also be used, for the purpose of threshold searches, to index a marked set of network nodes which has been assigned a negative weight. This does not affect the threshold search algorithm which evaluates the sum of the weights at a cluster node before passing through it. In the final version of the Capture system, however, negative weights were not used. For a system in which exclusions and negative weights are sufficiently important, it may be worthwhile (although this was not considered to be the case for the present system) always to index marked sets with and-markers as well as or-markers.

8.2. Clustering for the indexing scheme

For the searches which I have described the gain from using the clustering comes from excluding areas of the network which need not be searched. The size of this gain depends in part on how clustering correlates with marked sets; hence the interest in clustering criteria. The four clustering criteria which were tried in the Capture implementation can be referred to as the "creation", "specialization", "association", and "random" methods respectively. Each of these methods determines how nodes are clustered to form the indexing tree. More precisely, a clustering method determines the order in which network nodes are selected for placing them into clusters when the indexing tree is being built by the procedure described earlier in Section 8.1. The methods also determine how to incorporate new memory entities into this tree when these are created as a result of text processing.

The different clustering methods do not affect the final results of memory retrieval and search. This is because the search procedures use the indexing tree only to avoid searching areas of the network that are guaranteed not to include any result nodes (even though these areas may be different for different clustering methods). Hence we need not worry here about the formal properties of such a clustering, only the efficiency to be gained from it. The gain in efficiency derived from the indexing scheme is, as I remarked above, improved if marked sets are well correlated with (as opposed to sparsely distributed among) the clusters. The intention, except for the "random" method, is to have "semantic" criteria for clustering which improve the correlation between marked sets and clusters.

In the "creation" method the order in which the entities are chosen for inclusion into clusters is the same as the order in which the entities are created. The majority of the entities in memory are assumed to be created as a result of processing input files written by the person constructing the knowledge base. The order of memory assertions in these files would then presumably tend to clump semantically "close" information together, reflecting the constructor's model of the knowledge being represented.

Both the "specialization" (or "classification") and the "association" methods depend on specialization and correspondence assertions. The clustering order for the methods is the same as the order in which nodes are located by two different types of exhaustive traversal of the network formed by the links representing memory assertions. In the specialization method the traversal is a depth-first search of the network using specialization links and also role-specialization links (i.e. those that link the specialized-role and generic-role arguments of correspondence assertions). For the association method the traversal is a depth-first search which mainly uses the owner-role links from correspondence assertions, though it also uses specialization links because the chains of owner-role links do not span the whole network. Thus for the specialization method entities that are similar (as determined by the classification imposed by the specialization hierarchy) tend to be in the same clusters; whereas for the association method entities that are closely associated (via the owner-role relationships imposed by correspondence assertions) tend to be in the same clusters.

In addition to the three clustering methods just described, random clustering was implemented for the purpose of comparison. This method uses a pseudo-random number generator to ensure that there is no systematic semantic relationship between entities that are placed in the same clusters. Timing tests confirmed the expected result that random clustering was the least efficient. The specialization method appears to be the most efficient, followed by the association and creation methods respectively. Because of this the system was normally run using the specialization clustering option. An appropriate semantic clustering should become more advantageous than random clustering as the number of entities in memory increases. But I should add that it is not necessarily true that there is such an appropriate semantic clustering which could be used in conjunction with a very large memory knowledge base and an arbitrary pattern of processing performed on it. It is, however, more likely that a better than random clustering method could be found if processing the knowledge base follows a more restricted pattern of use, such as that required for performing certain very common interpretation operations.

In the case of the particular memory knowledge base used by Capture it turned out to be fairly easy to determine by trial and error a good initial cluster size (4) for minimizing the number of nodes visited during searches. There was also a fixed limit on the maximum size to which a cluster would be allowed to grow as a result of new memory entities being created and incorporated in existing clusters.

When a new entity is created, the system must choose the cluster into which it will be incorporated. The choice of cluster is determined by a function which is consistent with the clustering method being applied. For example, for specialization clustering a cluster which includes a generalization of the entity is chosen, otherwise, if there is no such cluster, a cluster including a role-generalization of the new entity is chosen. When the maximum size is exceeded for a particular cluster, a new cluster is created near the old one in the cluster tree. Of course, the whole network could be reclustered after a large number of updates takes place, but this was not done automatically by the Capture system.

Figures 8.2 and 8.3 below show for two example texts how the number of nodes visited during search operations varied with the clustering method and the cluster size used. It should be emphasized that the information given in these figures is only intended to give a general impression of how the various clustering methods affected memory searches for the relatively small memory knowledge base (around 450 entities) used by the test implementation. The size of the knowledge base means that it is still not clear how effective different clustering methods are, but it can be expected that the gains from applying semantic clustering methods to large knowledge bases would be greater than the modest (though consistent) gains shown here. The nodes counted include both entity nodes and indexing nodes visited during searches performed for processing the two example texts. These are the example texts given in Chapter 5 (i.e. texts A30 and A14 in Appendix A). The maximum cluster size (i.e. the size to which clusters are allowed to grow when new entities are created) is, in each case, 1.5 times the initial cluster size indicated.

8.3. Propagations in very large networks

Despite the use of the indexing scheme for implementing memory searches and the use of recorded propagations, the cost of marking large areas with temporary markers for very large networks will still be high. An extension of the indexing scheme for use with very large networks is therefore considered. This is aimed at reducing the marking effort during propagate/intersect algorithms. The extension was not included in the implemented system because it was felt that, given the size of the experimental knowledge base, it would not lead to any discernible increase in processing efficiency. However, the aim of the extension is to perform "approximate" marker propagations on a high level of the cluster tree and then use the information gained in this way to perform restricted propagations, only where necessary, on the network itself.

This would require the introduction of "cluster links" between the cluster nodes as follows. If one or more pairs of nodes in different clusters are linked by some link type, then a cluster link of the same type would be created between the respective cluster nodes. Propagations that use these cluster links are approximate in the sense that a cluster link does not imply the existence of a network link between any two particular network nodes.

For each of the network propagations that we wish to avoid performing, an approximate propagation is performed instead at the higher level using the corresponding links. A desired combination of markers on a cluster node means that the nodes in that cluster might be in the desired set. The paths leading to the cluster nodes with this combination can then be traced back to the sources of

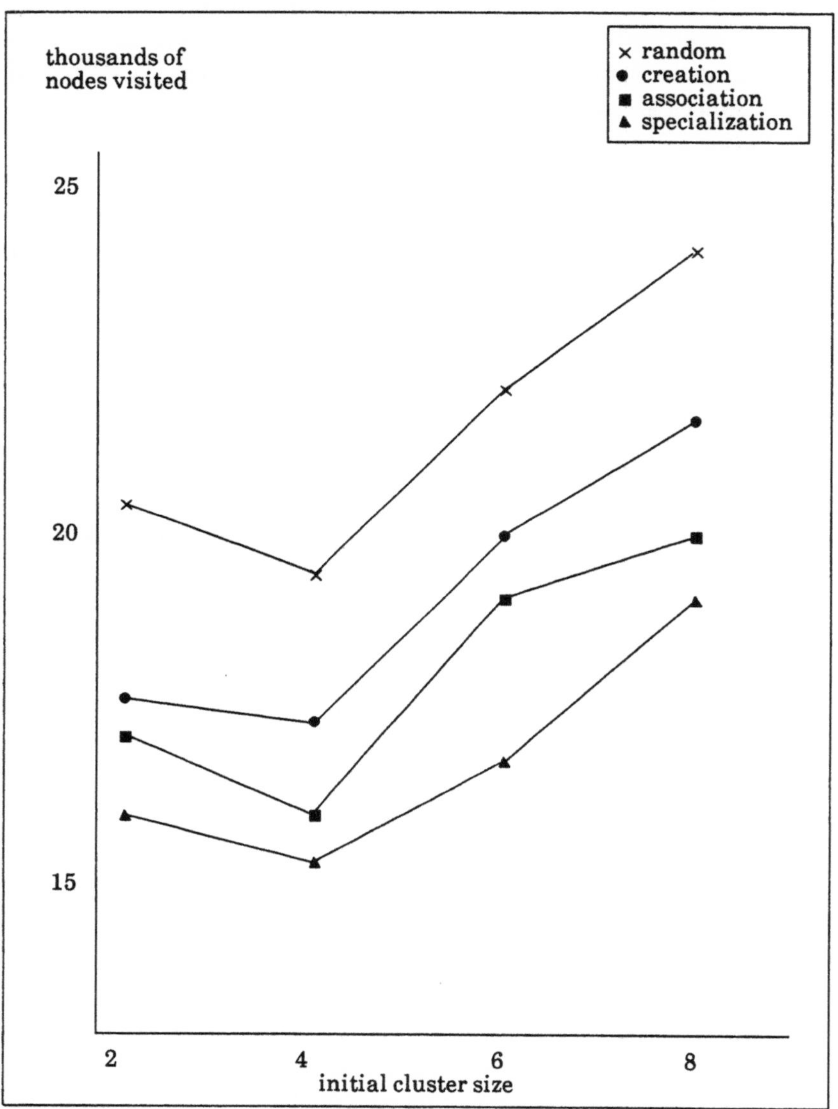

Figure 8.2. Effect of clustering methods on processing text A30

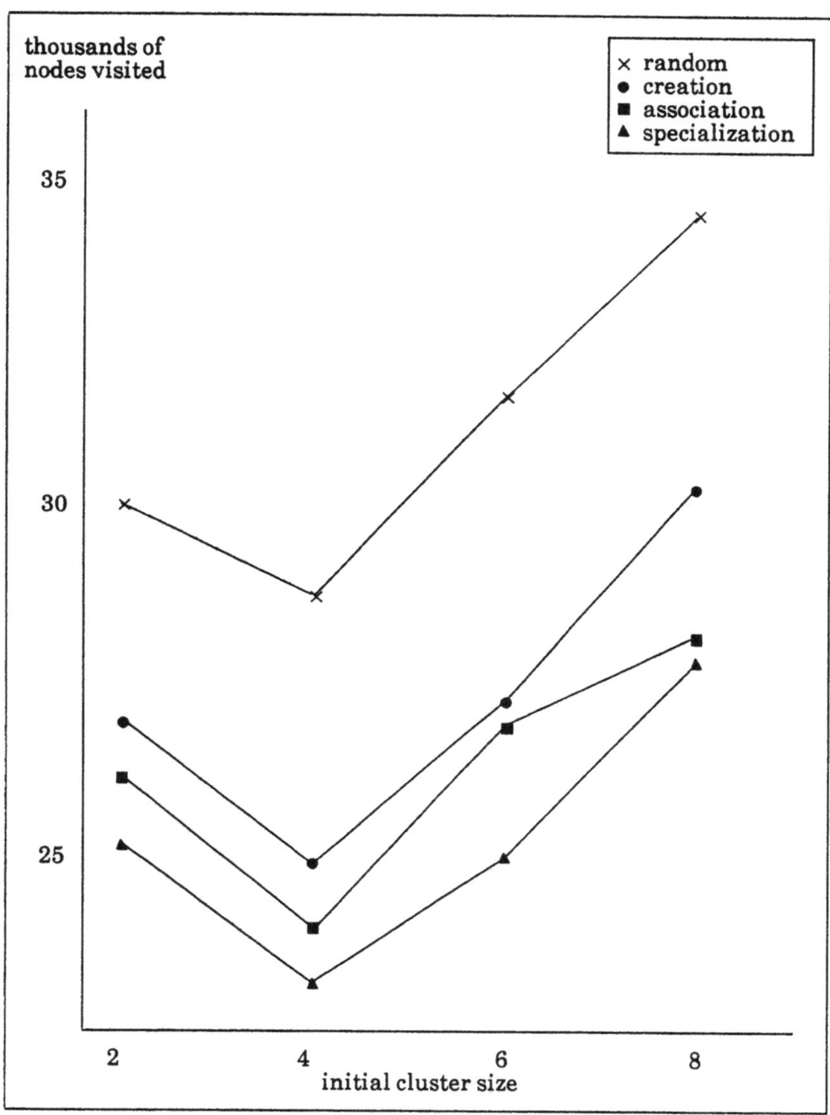

Figure 8.3. Effect of clustering methods on processing text A14

the marker propagations. The network nodes included in these paths would then be marked with special "pass" markers. Restricted propagations could then be performed on the main network by going through nodes which have pass markers. This would lead to marking all the nodes in the desired intersection, and should restrict marker spreading in the main network considerably.

Some other enhancements

Apart from the extension just described, other obvious efficiency enhancements are possible, such as the replacement of the lists used for indicating the set of markers on a node by bit vectors or AVL trees. This kind of very low level efficiency enhancement was not considered to be interesting enough for inclusion in an experimental system. It would be interesting, however, to try to record some of the propagations which start at a set of nodes, rather than restricting recorded propagations to those which start at a single node. However, maintaining these recorded propagations would be more complicated because the sets from which they start can change during memory processing.

As far as clustering is concerned, a possibility which is worth investigating is that of using the specialization hierarchy derived from memory assertions directly as the search tree. (This was suggested to me by Graeme Ritchie in personal communication.) Indexing markers would have to be distinguished from ordinary markers in this case. The scheme would have the advantages of not requiring additional storage space for the indexing tree, and of providing good correlation between the "clustering" and some important marked sets. Control over the cluster size, however, is not possible. There is also the complication that the memory hierarchies can branch upwards, which entails lower efficiency, or the need to restrict indexing to a minimum spanning tree.

All the implemented techniques and the suggestions in this chapter for improving the efficiency of memory retrieval have, as stated earlier, the property that they do not affect the outcome of retrieval operations. A different class of techniques which may be useful are those which depend on further information for determining, in a possibly error-prone way, sets of entities that can be ignored during the retrieval process. It was suggested in Section 4.2 that the activation values provided by the context mechanism might be used in this way.

8.4. Efficiency analysis of the intersection search

For the purpose of efficiency comparisons on memory processing, primitive operations can be defined as the operations of marking a node, testing the marks on a node against a marker combination, and calculating the activation of a node. If we assume that the time taken to perform one of these operations on a node (in the network or tree) is a small constant, we can then estimate the computational complexity of the searches by determining the number of nodes which are examined during a search.

The simple intersection case (i.e. looking for all the network nodes that are marked by all the markers in a specified combination) only will be analyzed. This case can be considered a special case of the threshold search since it is equivalent to finding nodes with weights that are greater than $k\text{-}1$ where k is the number of the markers in the combination, all of which have been assigned a weight equal to one, other markers having been assigned a weight equal to zero.

For the worst case of the intersection search, the number of nodes (in both network and tree) that are examined is of the same order as the number of nodes with the marker that marks the smallest set of network nodes in the intersection (the clustering factor being assumed to be a constant, c, for this analysis). Let m be the cardinality of this set. The number of nodes marked by this marker is less than the sum of the nodes in paths from the indexing root to each of the m nodes in the network. The length of these paths is $O(\log N)$ for a network with N nodes, and so the number of nodes marked by the marker and hence the number of nodes examined is $O(m \log N)$.

We can refine this upper bound for the worst case by observing that some of the nodes in the paths mentioned above must be shared near the top of the tree. Sharing need not occur below a level in the tree where there are more than m tree nodes, i.e. after a depth of $O(\log m)$ from the root. Thus the number of nodes marked will be bounded by the number of nodes above this level plus the (distinct) paths from this level to the network nodes. This gives

$$O(m) + O(m(\log N - \log m)), \text{ that is } O(m(\log(N/m))).$$

(Following the above analysis more closely, it can be seen that the constants are not unreasonable, a concrete bound being $2m + cm(\underline{\log}(N/m) + 1)$, where $\underline{\log}\ a$ is the largest integer less than or equal to the log of a to base c.) For the (good) case where we can assume that all tree nodes with the combination *do* lead to network nodes in the intersection, let the number of nodes in the intersection be i; the order of nodes examined will be the same as the order of nodes with the combination, giving $O(i \log(N/i))$ by the above analysis. For the (best) case, in which the number of nodes marked with the combination will be the number of nodes in a full c-branching tree with i leaves plus a path from the root to this tree, we get

$$O(i) + O(\log N - \log i), \text{ that is } O(i + \log(N/i)).$$

(Again the constants are reasonable, a concrete bound being $2i + c(\underline{\log}(N/i) + 1)$.)

As noted by Fahlman, the standard algorithm for finding the intersection of sets represented as lists takes at least $O(m)$, where m is the cardinality of the smallest set in the intersection (Fahlman 1979). This algorithm steps through the items on the shortest list checking for items in the intersection, this list being identified by maintaining counters for the number of items on each list. Thus, from the above analysis, this algorithm performs better than the cluster-based algorithm in the worst case, but the cluster-based algorithm can do better if the sets correlate well with the clustering. In addition, there is no obvious extension of the standard algorithm which can deal with the threshold search, which is important for our language interpretation framework. As I mentioned earlier, the threshold search is a generalization of the intersection search, and so it has at least the same computational complexity as the intersection search.

Appendix A
Example texts and output

This appendix contains the final output generated by the implemented system for a number of example texts for the Machines Database and for the Artifacts Database. The order in which these examples are presented roughly reflects the order in which they were used for testing as the system developed, so that the earlier examples in the appendix are simpler than the later ones which exhibit a wider range of interpretation problems. However, all the output given in this appendix was produced by exactly the same version of the system (using the same initial memory knowledge base) in September 1983. Typical times taken for the processing of each sentence in these texts are around 0.4 seconds for the analysis phase and a further 0.8 seconds for interleaved interpretation and task-specific processing; this includes Lisp garbage collection with the system running in about 1M bytes of store on an IBM 3081.

TEXT A01

JONES SUPPLIES P1234.
THE WEIGHT OF THE MACHINE IS 25.
THE STATUS OF THE SUPPLIER IS 10.
THE WEIGHT OF P6666 IS 25.
IT IS BLUE.

```
((SUPPLIES/RELATION ((SMC/MCNUM P1234) (SMC/SID Jones)))
 (MACHINES/RELATION ((MC/MCNUM P1234) (MC/WEIGHT 25)))
 (SUPPLIERS/RELATION ((S/SID Jones) (S/STATUS 10)))
 (MACHINES/RELATION ((MC/MCNUM P6666) (MC/WEIGHT 25)))
 (MACHINES/RELATION ((MC/MCNUM P6666) (MC/COLOR blue1))))
```

TEXT A02

P888 IS GREEN.
THE WEIGHT OF THE MACHINE IS 40.
SMITH SUPPLIES IT.
JONES SUPPLIES IT.
HE SUPPLIES P789.
THE STATUS OF THE SUPPLIER IS 15.
THE STATUS OF SMITH IS 20.
HE SUPPLIES P999.

```
((MACHINES/RELATION ((MC/MCNUM P888) (MC/COLOR green1)))
 (MACHINES/RELATION ((MC/MCNUM P888) (MC/WEIGHT 40)))
 (SUPPLIES/RELATION ((SMC/SID Smith1) (SMC/MCNUM P888)))
 (SUPPLIES/RELATION ((SMC/SID Jones) (SMC/MCNUM P888)))
 (SUPPLIES/RELATION ((SMC/MCNUM P789) (SMC/SID Jones)))
 (SUPPLIERS/RELATION ((S/SID Jones) (S/STATUS 15)))
 (SUPPLIERS/RELATION ((S/SID Smith1) (S/STATUS 20)))
 (SUPPLIES/RELATION ((SMC/MCNUM P999) (SMC/SID Smith1))))
```

TEXT A03

THE WEIGHT OF P4444 IS 24.
SMITH SUPPLIES IT.
THE STATUS OF THE SUPPLIER IS 10.
THE STATUS OF JONES IS 20.
HE SUPPLIES P9999.
THE MACHINE IS RED.
CLARK SUPPLIES IT.
ROBINSON SUPPLIES THE MACHINE WHICH IS SUPPLIED BY SMITH.
THE WEIGHT OF THE MACHINE THAT JONES SUPPLIES IS 29.

```
((MACHINES/RELATION ((MC/MCNUM P4444) (MC/WEIGHT 24)))
 (SUPPLIES/RELATION ((SMC/SID Smith1) (SMC/MCNUM P4444)))
 (SUPPLIERS/RELATION ((S/SID Smith1) (S/STATUS 10)))
 (SUPPLIERS/RELATION ((S/SID Jones) (S/STATUS 20)))
 (SUPPLIES/RELATION ((SMC/MCNUM P9999) (SMC/SID Jones)))
 (MACHINES/RELATION ((MC/MCNUM P9999) (MC/COLOR red1)))
 (SUPPLIES/RELATION ((SMC/SID Clark1) (SMC/MCNUM P9999)))
 (SUPPLIES/RELATION ((SMC/SID Robinson1) (SMC/MCNUM P4444)))
 (MACHINES/RELATION ((MC/MCNUM P9999) (MC/WEIGHT 29))))
```

TEXT A04

SMITH SUPPLIES P9999.
JONES SUPPLIES P4444.

THEY SUPPLY P7777.
THE MACHINES ARE RED.

```
((SUPPLIES/RELATION ((SMC/MCNUM P9999) (SMC/SID Smith1)))
 (SUPPLIES/RELATION ((SMC/MCNUM P4444) (SMC/SID Jones)))
 (SUPPLIES/RELATION ((SMC/MCNUM P7777) (SMC/SID Smith1)))
 (SUPPLIES/RELATION ((SMC/MCNUM P7777) (SMC/SID Jones)))
 (MACHINES/RELATION ((MC/COLOR red1) (MC/MCNUM P9999)))
 (MACHINES/RELATION ((MC/COLOR red1) (MC/MCNUM P4444)))
 (MACHINES/RELATION ((MC/COLOR red1) (MC/MCNUM P7777))))
```

TEXT A05

PHILIPS MANUFACTURES P4444.
IT IS RED.
THE COLOUR OF P4040 IS BLUE.
THE MACHINES ARE SUPPLIED BY SMITH.
JONES SUPPLIES P9999.
IT IS MADE BY MARCONI.
THE STATUS OF THE SUPPLIER IS 90.
THIS MACHINE IS GREEN.
CLARK SUPPLIES THE MACHINE WHICH IS MADE BY PHILIPS.
THE WEIGHT OF THE GREEN MACHINE IS 29.

```
((MANUFACTURES/RELATION ((M/MCNUM P4444) (M/MNAME Philips)))
 (MACHINES/RELATION ((MC/MCNUM P4444) (MC/COLOR red1)))
 (MACHINES/RELATION ((MC/MCNUM P4040) (MC/COLOR blue1)))
 (SUPPLIES/RELATION ((SMC/SID Smith1) (SMC/MCNUM P4444)))
 (SUPPLIES/RELATION ((SMC/SID Smith1) (SMC/MCNUM P4040)))
 (SUPPLIES/RELATION ((SMC/MCNUM P9999) (SMC/SID Jones)))
 (MANUFACTURES/RELATION ((M/MNAME Marconi) (M/MCNUM P9999)))
 (SUPPLIERS/RELATION ((S/SID Jones) (S/STATUS 90)))
 (MACHINES/RELATION ((MC/MCNUM P9999) (MC/COLOR green1)))
 (SUPPLIES/RELATION ((SMC/SID Clark1) (SMC/MCNUM P4444)))
 (MACHINES/RELATION ((MC/MCNUM P9999) (MC/WEIGHT 29))))
```

TEXT A06

MARCONI MANUFACTURES P9999.
PHILIPS MAKES P4444.
THE STATUS OF SMITH IS 50.
THE STATUS OF CLARK IS 80.
THEY SUPPLY THE MACHINES.

```
((MANUFACTURES/RELATION ((M/MCNUM P9999) (M/MNAME Marconi)))
 (MANUFACTURES/RELATION ((M/MCNUM P4444) (M/MNAME Philips)))
 (SUPPLIERS/RELATION ((S/SID Smith1) (S/STATUS 50)))
 (SUPPLIERS/RELATION ((S/SID Clark1) (S/STATUS 80)))
 (SUPPLIES/RELATION ((SMC/MCNUM P9999) (SMC/SID Smith1)))
 (SUPPLIES/RELATION ((SMC/MCNUM P9999) (SMC/SID Clark1)))
 (SUPPLIES/RELATION ((SMC/MCNUM P4444) (SMC/SID Smith1)))
 (SUPPLIES/RELATION ((SMC/MCNUM P4444) (SMC/SID Clark1))))
```

TEXT A07

P9999 IS GREEN.
P7777 IS RED.
JONES SUPPLIES THE MACHINES.
P8888 IS RED.
MARCONI MANUFACTURES THE MACHINES THAT ARE SUPPLIED BY JONES.
PHILIPS MANUFACTURES THE RED MACHINES.

```
((MACHINES/RELATION ((MC/MCNUM P9999) (MC/COLOR green1)))
  (MACHINES/RELATION ((MC/MCNUM P7777) (MC/COLOR red1)))
  (SUPPLIES/RELATION ((SMC/SID Jones) (SMC/MCNUM P9999)))
  (SUPPLIES/RELATION ((SMC/SID Jones) (SMC/MCNUM P7777)))
  (MACHINES/RELATION ((MC/MCNUM P8888) (MC/COLOR red1)))
  (MANUFACTURES/RELATION ((M/MNAME Marconi) (M/MCNUM P9999)))
  (MANUFACTURES/RELATION ((M/MNAME Marconi) (M/MCNUM P7777)))
  (MANUFACTURES/RELATION ((M/MNAME Philips) (M/MCNUM P7777)))
  (MANUFACTURES/RELATION ((M/MNAME Philips) (M/MCNUM P8888))))
```

TEXT A08

MARCONI MANUFACTURES P9999.
IT IS SUPPLIED BY SMITH.
THE STATUS OF THE SUPPLIER IS 30.
THE STATUS OF JONES IS 40.
THEY SUPPLY P9900.
THIS MACHINE IS A COMPUTER.
IT IS MADE BY PHILIPS.
THE MACHINES ARE RED.
THE COLOUR OF P4444 IS GREEN.
THE COMPUTER MANUFACTURER MAKES THE GREEN MACHINE.
P9000 IS BLUE.
IT IS A DISC-DRIVE.
IT IS SUPPLIED BY THE STATUS 30 SUPPLIER.
HE GAVE P8888 TO THE P9999 MANUFACTURER.
THE DISC-DRIVE IS MADE BY THIS MANUFACTURER.
THE WEIGHT OF THE MACHINES THAT ARE MADE BY MARCONI IS 35.

```
((MANUFACTURES/RELATION ((M/MCNUM P9999) (M/MNAME Marconi)))
  (SUPPLIES/RELATION ((SMC/SID Smith1) (SMC/MCNUM P9999)))
  (SUPPLIERS/RELATION ((S/SID Smith1) (S/STATUS 30)))
  (SUPPLIERS/RELATION ((S/SID Jones) (S/STATUS 40)))
  (SUPPLIES/RELATION ((SMC/MCNUM P9900) (SMC/SID Smith1)))
  (SUPPLIES/RELATION ((SMC/MCNUM P9900) (SMC/SID Jones)))
  (MACHINES/RELATION ((MC/TYPE computer) (MC/MCNUM P9900)))
  (MANUFACTURES/RELATION ((M/MNAME Philips) (M/MCNUM P9900)))
  (MACHINES/RELATION ((MC/COLOR red1) (MC/MCNUM P9999)))
  (MACHINES/RELATION ((MC/COLOR red1) (MC/MCNUM P9900)))
  (MACHINES/RELATION ((MC/MCNUM P4444) (MC/COLOR green1)))
  (MANUFACTURES/RELATION ((M/MCNUM P4444) (M/MNAME Philips)))
  (MACHINES/RELATION ((MC/MCNUM P9000) (MC/COLOR blue1)))
  (MACHINES/RELATION ((MC/TYPE disc-drive1) (MC/MCNUM P9000)))
  (SUPPLIES/RELATION ((SMC/MCNUM P9000) (SMC/SID Smith1)))
  (MANUFACTURES/RELATION ((M/MCNUM P9000) (M/MNAME Marconi)))
  (MACHINES/RELATION ((MC/WEIGHT 35) (MC/MCNUM P9999)))
  (MACHINES/RELATION ((MC/WEIGHT 35) (MC/MCNUM P9000))))
```

TEXT A09

MARCONI MANUFACTURES P9999.
IT IS SUPPLIED BY SMITH WHO SUPPLIES P7777 WHICH IS RED.
THE RED MACHINE IS MADE BY PHILIPS.
THE ONE THAT IS MADE BY MARCONI IS BLUE.

```
((MANUFACTURES/RELATION ((M/MCNUM P9999) (M/MNAME Marconi)))
  (MACHINES/RELATION ((MC/MCNUM P7777) (MC/COLOR red1)))
  (SUPPLIES/RELATION ((SMC/MCNUM P7777) (SMC/SID Smith1)))
  (SUPPLIES/RELATION ((SMC/SID Smith1) (SMC/MCNUM P9999)))
  (MANUFACTURES/RELATION ((M/MNAME Philips) (M/MCNUM P7777)))
  (MACHINES/RELATION ((MC/MCNUM P9999) (MC/COLOR blue1))))
```

TEXT A10

P7777 IS A COMPUTER THAT IS MANUFACTURED BY PHILIPS.
THE MANUFACTURER MAKES P7700 WHICH IS SUPPLIED BY SMITH.
JONES AND CLARK SUPPLY THE COMPUTER.
THE STATUS OF THE COMPUTER SUPPLIERS IS 20.

```
((MANUFACTURES/RELATION ((M/MNAME Philips) (M/MCNUM P7777)))
  (MACHINES/RELATION ((MC/TYPE computer) (MC/MCNUM P7777)))
  (SUPPLIES/RELATION ((SMC/SID Smith1) (SMC/MCNUM P7700)))
  (MANUFACTURES/RELATION ((M/MCNUM P7700) (M/MNAME Philips)))
  (SUPPLIES/RELATION ((SMC/MCNUM P7777) (SMC/SID Clark1)))
  (SUPPLIES/RELATION ((SMC/MCNUM P7777) (SMC/SID Jones)))
  (SUPPLIERS/RELATION ((S/STATUS 20) (S/SID Clark1)))
  (SUPPLIERS/RELATION ((S/STATUS 20) (S/SID Jones))))
```

TEXT A11

MARCONI MANUFACTURES P9999 WHICH IS A DISC-DRIVE.
IT IS SUPPLIED BY SMITH.
THE STATUS OF THE SUPPLIER IS 30.
THE STATUS OF JONES IS 40.
THEY SUPPLY P7777 WHICH IS MANUFACTURED BY PHILIPS.
IT IS A TERMINAL.
THESE MACHINES ARE RED.

P9000 IS MANUFACTURED BY MARCONI.
IT IS A BLUE PRINTER.
P4444 IS GREEN.
THE BLUE MACHINE IS SUPPLIED BY THE STATUS 30 SUPPLIER.
THE TERMINAL MANUFACTURER MAKES THE GREEN MACHINE.
THE WEIGHT OF THE MACHINES THAT ARE MADE BY MARCONI IS 35.

SMITH SUPPLIES P1010 WHICH IS A COMPUTER.
THIS ONE IS MANUFACTURED BY IBM.
THE SUPPLIER SUPPLIES P6200 WHICH IS MADE BY PHILIPS.
THE WEIGHT OF THE COMPUTER IS 75.

```
((MACHINES/RELATION ((MC/TYPE disc-drive1) (MC/MCNUM P9999)))
  (MANUFACTURES/RELATION ((M//MNAME Marconi) (M/MCNUM P9999)))
  (SUPPLIES/RELATION ((SMC/SID Smith1) (SMC/MCNUM P9999)))
  (SUPPLIERS/RELATION ((S/SID Smith1) (S/STATUS 30)))
  (SUPPLIERS/RELATION ((S/SID Jones) (S/STATUS 40)))
  (MANUFACTURES/RELATION ((M/MNAME Philips) (M/MCNUM P7777)))
  (SUPPLIES/RELATION ((SMC/MCNUM P7777) (SMC/SID Smith1)))
  (SUPPLIES/RELATION ((SMC/MCNUM P7777) (SMC/SID Jones)))
  (MACHINES/RELATION ((MC/TYPE terminal1) (MC/MCNUM P7777)))
  (MACHINES/RELATION ((MC/COLOR red1) (MC/MCNUM P9999)))
  (MACHINES/RELATION ((MC/COLOR red1) (MC/MCNUM P7777)))
  (MANUFACTURES/RELATION ((M/MCNUM P9000) (M/MNAME Marconi)))
  (MACHINES/RELATION ((MC/MCNUM P9000) (MC/COLOR blue1)))
  (MACHINES/RELATION ((MC/TYPE printer2) (MC/MCNUM P9000)))
  (MACHINES/RELATION ((MC/MCNUM P4444) (MC/COLOR green1)))
  (SUPPLIES/RELATION ((SMC/MCNUM P9000) (SMC/SID Smith1)))
  (MANUFACTURES/RELATION ((M/MCNUM P4444) (M/MNAME Philips)))
  (MACHINES/RELATION ((MC/WEIGHT 35) (MC/MCNUM P9999)))
  (MACHINES/RELATION ((MC/WEIGHT 35) (MC/MCNUM P9000)))
  (MACHINES/RELATION ((MC/TYPE computer) (MC/MCNUM P1010)))
  (SUPPLIES/RELATION ((SMC/SID Smith1) (SMC/MCNUM P1010)))
  (MANUFACTURES/RELATION ((M/MNAME IBM) (M/MCNUM P1010)))
  (MANUFACTURES/RELATION ((M/MCNUM P6200) (M/MNAME Philips)))
```

```
(SUPPLIES/RELATION ((SMC/MCNUM P6200) (SMC/SID Smith1)))
(MACHINES/RELATION ((MC/MCNUM P1010) (MC/WEIGHT 75))))
```

TEXT A12

P7777 IS A COMPUTER.
IT IS MANUFACTURED BY PHILIPS.
P9920 IS A DISC-DRIVE THAT IS MANUFACTURED BY MARCONI.
THIS MANUFACTURER MAKES P9999 WHICH IS SUPPLIED BY JONES.
SMITH SUPPLIES THE COMPUTER.
THE STATUS OF P7777'S SUPPLIER IS 20.

```
((MACHINES/RELATION ((MC/TYPE computer) (MC/MCNUM P7777)))
 (MANUFACTURES/RELATION ((M/MNAME Philips) (M/MCNUM P7777)))
 (MANUFACTURES/RELATION ((M/MNAME Marconi) (M/MCNUM P9920)))
 (MACHINES/RELATION ((MC/TYPE disc-drive1) (MC/MCNUM P9920)))
 (SUPPLIES/RELATION ((SMC/SID Jones) (SMC/MCNUM P9999)))
 (MANUFACTURES/RELATION ((M/MCNUM P9999) (M/MNAME Marconi)))
 (SUPPLIES/RELATION ((SMC/SID Smith1) (SMC/MCNUM P7777)))
 (SUPPLIERS/RELATION ((S/SID Smith1) (S/STATUS 20))))
```

TEXT A13

P9999 IS A MAIN-FRAME THAT IS SUPPLIED BY SMITH.
HE SUPPLIES P7777 WHICH IS A TERMINAL.
JONES SUPPLIES P7700.
IT IS A DISC-DRIVE.
MARCONI MANUFACTURES THE COMPUTER IN PARIS.
THE PERIPHERALS ARE MADE BY PHILIPS.

```
((SUPPLIES/RELATION ((SMC/SID Smith1) (SMC/MCNUM P9999)))
 (MACHINES/RELATION ((MC/TYPE computer) (MC/MCNUM P9999)))
 (MACHINES/RELATION ((MC/TYPE terminal1) (MC/MCNUM P7777)))
 (SUPPLIES/RELATION ((SMC/SID Smith1) (SMC/MCNUM P7777)))
 (SUPPLIES/RELATION ((SMC/MCNUM P7700) (SMC/SID Jones)))
 (MACHINES/RELATION ((MC/TYPE disc-drive1) (MC/MCNUM P7700)))
 (MANUFACTURES/RELATION
        ((M/MNAME Marconi) (M/MCNUM P9999) (M/CITY Paris)))
 (MANUFACTURES/RELATION ((M/MNAME Philips) (M/MCNUM P7777)))
 (MANUFACTURES/RELATION ((M/MNAME Philips) (M/MCNUM P7700))))
```

TEXT A14

PLEXIR MANUFACTURES P9999 WHICH IS A COMPUTER.
IT IS SUPPLIED BY SMITH.
P1010 IS A TERMINAL THAT IS SUPPLIED BY CLARK.
THIS ONE IS MADE BY MIKOTA.
THESE MACHINES ARE RED.

P9000 IS A GREEN PRINTER.
IT IS MADE BY PLEXIR.
P4444 IS A BLUE COMPUTER.
THE COST OF THE MACHINE IS 7850.
THE PERIPHERAL IS SUPPLIED BY THE P9999 SUPPLIER.
THE TERMINAL MANUFACTURER MAKES THE BLUE MACHINE.
THE COST OF MIKOTA'S PERIPHERAL IS 235.

```
((MACHINES/RELATION ((MC/TYPE computer) (MC/MCNUM P9999)))
 (MANUFACTURES/RELATION ((M/MNAME Plexir1) (M/MCNUM P9999)))
 (SUPPLIES/RELATION ((SMC/SID Smith1) (SMC/MCNUM P9999)))
 (SUPPLIES/RELATION ((SMC/SID Clark1) (SMC/MCNUM P1010)))
 (MACHINES/RELATION ((MC/TYPE terminal1) (MC/MCNUM P1010)))
```

```
(MANUFACTURES/RELATION ((M/MNAME Mikota1) (M/MCNUM P1010)))
(MACHINES/RELATION ((MC/COLOR red1) (MC/MCNUM P9999)))
(MACHINES/RELATION ((MC/COLOR red1) (MC/MCNUM P1010)))
(MACHINES/RELATION ((MC/MCNUM P9000) (MC/COLOR green1)))
(MACHINES/RELATION ((MC/TYPE printer2) (MC/MCNUM P9000)))
(MANUFACTURES/RELATION ((M/MNAME Plexir1) (M/MCNUM P9000)))
(MACHINES/RELATION ((MC/MCNUM P4444) (MC/COLOR blue1)))
(MACHINES/RELATION ((MC/TYPE computer) (MC/MCNUM P4444)))
(MACHINES/RELATION ((MC/MCNUM P4444) (MC/COST 7850)))
(SUPPLIES/RELATION ((SMC/SID Smith1) (SMC/MCNUM P9000)))
(MANUFACTURES/RELATION ((M/MNAME Mikota1) (M/MCNUM P4444)))
(MACHINES/RELATION ((MC/MCNUM P1010) (MC/COST 235))))
```

TEXT A15

P8880 IS A COMPUTER THAT IS MANUFACTURED BY MIKOTA.
THE COST OF THE MACHINE IS 2595.

P7770 IS MANUFACTURED BY PLEXIR.
MARCONI MAKES P7200.
THE COST OF BOTH MACHINES IS 4000.

```
((MANUFACTURES/RELATION ((M/MNAME Mikota1) (M/MCNUM P8880)))
 (MACHINES/RELATION ((MC/TYPE computer) (MC/MCNUM P8880)))
 (MACHINES/RELATION ((MC/MCNUM P8880) (MC/COST 2595)))
 (MANUFACTURES/RELATION ((M/MNAME Plexir1) (M/MCNUM P7770)))
 (MANUFACTURES/RELATION ((M/MCNUM P7200) (M/MNAME Marconi)))
 (MACHINES/RELATION ((MC/COST 4000) (MC/MCNUM P7200)))
 (MACHINES/RELATION ((MC/COST 4000) (MC/MCNUM P7770))))
```

TEXT A16

P8080 IS SUPPLIED BY PETERS.
THE STATUS OF THE SUPPLIER IS 20.

CLARK SUPPLIES P7780 AND P7790.
P7720 IS SUPPLIED BY ROBINSON.
THESE THREE MACHINES ARE MANUFACTURED BY PLEXIR.

```
((SUPPLIES/RELATION ((SMC/SID Peters1) (SMC/MCNUM P8080)))
 (SUPPLIERS/RELATION ((S/SID Peters1) (S/STATUS 20)))
 (SUPPLIES/RELATION ((SMC/SID Clark1) (SMC/MCNUM P7790)))
 (SUPPLIES/RELATION ((SMC/SID Clark1) (SMC/MCNUM P7780)))
 (SUPPLIES/RELATION ((SMC/SID Robinson1) (SMC/MCNUM P7720)))
 (MANUFACTURES/RELATION ((M/MNAME Plexir1) (M/MCNUM P7780)))
 (MANUFACTURES/RELATION ((M/MNAME Plexir1) (M/MCNUM P7790)))
 (MANUFACTURES/RELATION ((M/MNAME Plexir1) (M/MCNUM P7720))))
```

TEXT A17

P9999 IS A DISC-DRIVE THAT IS SUPPLIED BY SMITH.
THIS PERIPHERAL IS MANUFACTURED BY MIKOTA.
HE SUPPLIES P7777 WHICH IS A TERMINAL.
IT IS MANUFACTURED IN LONDON BY PLEXIR.
CLARK SUPPLIES P9000 WHICH IS MANUFACTURED BY MARCONI IN PARIS.

```
((SUPPLIES/RELATION ((SMC/SID Smith1) (SMC/MCNUM P9999)))
 (MACHINES/RELATION ((MC/TYPE disc-drive1) (MC/MCNUM P9999)))
 (MANUFACTURES/RELATION ((M/MNAME Mikota1) (M/MCNUM P9999)))
 (MACHINES/RELATION ((MC/TYPE terminal1) (MC/MCNUM P7777)))
 (SUPPLIES/RELATION ((SMC/SID Smith1) (SMC/MCNUM P7777)))
 (MANUFACTURES/RELATION
        ((M/MNAME Plexir1) (M/MCNUM P7777) (M/CITY London)))
```

```
(MANUFACTURES/RELATION
        ((M/MNAME Marconi) (M/MCNUM P9000) (M/CITY Paris)))
(SUPPLIES/RELATION ((SMC/MCNUM P9000) (SMC/SID Clark1))))
```

TEXT A18

WINTRON MANUFACTURES P5050 WHICH IS A DISC-DRIVE.
P1010 IS A COMPUTER WHICH IS MADE BY THIS MANUFACTURER.
IT HAS A BOLT.
P8770 IS A PRINTER THAT IS MADE BY PLEXIR.
BOTH PERIPHERALS ARE SUPPLIED BY CLARK.
SMITH SUPPLIES THE MACHINE WITH THE BOLT.

P4740 IS MANUFACTURED BY P5050'S MANUFACTURER IN LONDON.
IT IS A MICRO-COMPUTER THAT IS SUPPLIED BY JONES.
HE SUPPLIES P8800 WHICH IS A TERMINAL.
THE COST OF THE COMPUTER IS 25.
THE COMPUTERS ARE RED.
THE THREE PERIPHERALS ARE GREEN.

```
((MACHINES/RELATION ((MC/TYPE disc-drive1) (MC/MCNUM P5050)))
 (MANUFACTURES/RELATION ((M/MNAME Wintron1) (M/MCNUM P5050)))
 (MANUFACTURES/RELATION ((M/MNAME Wintron1) (M/MCNUM P1010)))
 (MACHINES/RELATION ((MC/TYPE computer) (MC/MCNUM P1010)))
 (MANUFACTURES/RELATION ((M/MNAME Plexir1) (M/MCNUM P8770)))
 (MACHINES/RELATION ((MC/TYPE printer2) (MC/MCNUM P8770)))
 (SUPPLIES/RELATION ((SMC/SID Clark1) (SMC/MCNUM P5050)))
 (SUPPLIES/RELATION ((SMC/SID Clark1) (SMC/MCNUM P8770)))
 (SUPPLIES/RELATION ((SMC/SID Smith1) (SMC/MCNUM P1010)))
 (MANUFACTURES/RELATION
        ((M/MCNUM P4740) (M/MNAME Wintron1) (M/CITY London)))
 (SUPPLIES/RELATION ((SMC/SID Jones) (SMC/MCNUM P4740)))
 (MACHINES/RELATION ((MC/TYPE computer) (MC/MCNUM P4740)))
 (MACHINES/RELATION ((MC/TYPE terminal1) (MC/MCNUM P8800)))
 (SUPPLIES/RELATION ((SMC/SID Jones) (SMC/MCNUM P8800)))
 (MACHINES/RELATION ((MC/MCNUM P4740) (MC/COST 25)))
 (MACHINES/RELATION ((MC/COLOR red1) (MC/MCNUM P1010)))
 (MACHINES/RELATION ((MC/COLOR red1) (MC/MCNUM P4740)))
 (MACHINES/RELATION ((MC/COLOR green1) (MC/MCNUM P5050)))
 (MACHINES/RELATION ((MC/COLOR green1) (MC/MCNUM P8770)))
 (MACHINES/RELATION ((MC/COLOR green1) (MC/MCNUM P8800))))
```

TEXT A19

PLEXIR MANUFACTURES P7777 WHICH IS COMPUTER.
IT HAS A SCREW.
WINTRON MAKES P9999 WHICH HAS A BOLT.
THE COST OF THE MACHINE WITH THE SCREW IS 9000.
THE MACHINE THAT HAS THE BOLT IS SUPPLIED BY CLARK.

```
((MACHINES/RELATION ((MC/TYPE computer) (MC/MCNUM P7777)))
 (MANUFACTURES/RELATION ((M/MNAME Plexir1) (M/MCNUM P7777)))
 (MANUFACTURES/RELATION ((M/MNAME Wintron1) (M/MCNUM P9999)))
 (MACHINES/RELATION ((MC/MCNUM P7777) (MC/COST 9000)))
 (SUPPLIES/RELATION ((SMC/SID Clark1) (SMC/MCNUM P9999))))
```

TEXT A20

PLEXIR MANUFACTURES P9000.
IT IS A MICRO-COMPUTER.
WINTRON MANUFACTURES P7000 WHICH IS A DISC-DRIVE.
P9000 IS SUPPLIED BY SMITH.

P8000 IS A COMPUTER.
IT IS SUPPLIED BY JONES.
THE STATUS OF THIS SUPPLIER IS 10.
THE STATUS OF P9000'S SUPPLIER IS 20.
THE MICRO-COMPUTER IS RED.
THE MANUFACTURER MANUFACTURES P9090.

```
((MANUFACTURES/RELATION ((M/MCNUM P9000) (M/MNAME Plexir1)))
 (MACHINES/RELATION ((MC/TYPE computer) (MC/MCNUM P9000)))
 (MACHINES/RELATION ((MC/TYPE disc-drive1) (MC/MCNUM P7000)))
 (MANUFACTURES/RELATION ((M/MNAME Wintron1) (M/MCNUM P7000)))
 (SUPPLIES/RELATION ((SMC/SID Smith1) (SMC/MCNUM P9000)))
 (MACHINES/RELATION ((MC/TYPE computer) (MC/MCNUM P8000)))
 (SUPPLIES/RELATION ((SMC/SID Jones) (SMC/MCNUM P8000)))
 (SUPPLIERS/RELATION ((S/SID Jones) (S/STATUS 10)))
 (SUPPLIERS/RELATION ((S/SID Smith1) (S/STATUS 20)))
 (MACHINES/RELATION ((MC/MCNUM P9000) (MC/COLOR red1)))
 (MANUFACTURES/RELATION ((M/MCNUM P9090) (M/MNAME Plexir1))))
```

TEXT A21

HADDON COLLECTED P33 WHICH IS AN ARMLET.
HE COLLECTED P37 FROM WOODLARK.
IT IS A NECKLACE.

BEVAN DONATED P571 AND P352.
P571 IS A SKIRT.
P352 IS A NECKLACE.
BEVAN COLLECTED BOTH ARTIFACTS AT MOUNT-HAGEN.

P576 IS FRAGILE.
HADDON DONATED IT TO LAMBERTS.
P220 IS A HARD BOX.

```
((ARTIFACTS/RELATION ((ARTF/TYPE ornament1) (ARTF/NUMB P33)))
 (ORIGIN/RELATION ((ORIG/COLL Haddon1) (ORIG/ARTN P33)))
 (ORIGIN/RELATION ((ORIG/ARTN P37) (ORIG/COLL Haddon1) (ORIG/PLAC Woodlark)))
 (ARTIFACTS/RELATION ((ARTF/TYPE ornament1) (ARTF/NUMB P37)))
 (ARTIFACTS/RELATION ((ARTF/TYPE clothing1) (ARTF/NUMB P571)))
 (ARTIFACTS/RELATION ((ARTF/TYPE ornament1) (ARTF/NUMB P352)))
 (ORIGIN/RELATION
       ((ORIG/PLAC Mount-Hagen) (ORIG/COLL Bevan1) (ORIG/ARTN P571)))
 (ORIGIN/RELATION
       ((ORIG/PLAC Mount-Hagen) (ORIG/COLL Bevan1) (ORIG/ARTN P352)))
 (ARTIFACTS/RELATION ((ARTF/NUMB P576) (ARTF/COND fragile1)))
 (ARTIFACTS/RELATION ((ARTF/NUMB P220) (ARTF/COND hard1)))
 (ARTIFACTS/RELATION ((ARTF/TYPE container1) (ARTF/NUMB P220))))
```

TEXT A22

P4830 IS A CANOE-PROW.
IT WAS DONATED BY HADDON.
HE COLLECTED IT IN DAUI.
BEVAN COLLECTED P981 WHICH IS A CANOE MODEL FROM WOODLARK.
BOTH ARTIFACTS ARE FRAGILE.

```
((ARTIFACTS/RELATION ((ARTF/TYPE navigation/artifact) (ARTF/NUMB P4830)))
 (ORIGIN/RELATION ((ORIG/ARTN P4830) (ORIG/PLAC Daui) (ORIG/COLL Haddon1)))
 (ARTIFACTS/RELATION ((ARTF/TYPE model1) (ARTF/NUMB P981)))
 (ORIGIN/RELATION ((ORIG/COLL Bevan1) (ORIG/ARTN P981) (ORIG/PLAC Woodlark)))
 (ARTIFACTS/RELATION ((ARTF/COND fragile1) (ARTF/NUMB P981)))
 (ARTIFACTS/RELATION ((ARTF/COND fragile1) (ARTF/NUMB P4830))))
```

TEXT A23

P562 IS A POT THAT WAS DONATED BY HADDON.
THE CONDITION OF THE POT IS GOOD.
HE COLLECTED IT FROM WOODLARK.
P371 WAS COLLECTED BY BEVAN FROM THERE.
THIS ARTIFACT IS AN ARMLET.

```
((ARTIFACTS/RELATION ((ARTF/TYPE container1) (ARTF/NUMB P562)))
  (ARTIFACTS/RELATION ((ARTF/NUMB P562) (ARTF/COND good1)))
  (ORIGIN/RELATION ((ORIG/ARTN P562) (ORIG/PLAC Woodlark) (ORIG/COLL Haddon1)))
  (ORIGIN/RELATION ((ORIG/COLL Bevan1) (ORIG/ARTN P371) (ORIG/PLAC Woodlark)))
  (ARTIFACTS/RELATION ((ARTF/TYPE ornament1) (ARTF/NUMB P371))))
```

TEXT A24

P20 IS A PADDLE THAT WAS COLLECTED FROM WOODLARK.
P70 WAS COLLECTED IN NEW-GUINEA.
THE WOODLARK ARTIFACT WAS COLLECTED BY ARMSTRONG.
HADDON COLLECTED P70.
THE CONDITION OF THESE ARTIFACTS IS GOOD.
ARMSTRONG'S PADDLE IS SMALL.

```
((ORIGIN/RELATION ((ORIG/ARTN P20) (ORIG/PLAC Woodlark)))
  (ARTIFACTS/RELATION ((ARTF/TYPE navigation/artifact) (ARTF/NUMB P20)))
  (ORIGIN/RELATION ((ORIG/ARTN P70) (ORIG/PLAC New-Guinea)))
  (ORIGIN/RELATION ((ORIG/COLL Armstrong1) (ORIG/ARTN P20)))
  (ORIGIN/RELATION ((ORIG/COLL Haddon1) (ORIG/ARTN P70)))
  (ARTIFACTS/RELATION ((ARTF/COND good1) (ARTF/NUMB P20)))
  (ARTIFACTS/RELATION ((ARTF/COND good1) (ARTF/NUMB P70))))
```

TEXT A25

HADDON COLLECTED P590 WHICH IS A POT.
HE COLLECTED P520.
IT IS A CANOE WITH A PADDLE.
BOTH ARTIFACTS COME FROM NEW-GUINEA.
BEVAN COLLECTED P422.
THIS ARTIFACT IS A LARGE JUG WITH A LID.
THE CONDITION OF THE HADDON CONTAINER IS GOOD.
THE ONE THAT WAS COLLECTED BY BEVAN IS FRAGILE.

```
((ARTIFACTS/RELATION ((ARTF/TYPE container1) (ARTF/NUMB P590)))
  (ORIGIN/RELATION ((ORIG/COLL Haddon1) (ORIG/ARTN P590)))
  (ORIGIN/RELATION ((ORIG/ARTN P520) (ORIG/COLL Haddon1)))
  (ARTIFACTS/RELATION ((ARTF/TYPE navigation/artifact) (ARTF/NUMB P520)))
  (ORIGIN/RELATION ((ORIG/PLAC New-Guinea) (ORIG/ARTN P590)))
  (ORIGIN/RELATION ((ORIG/PLAC New-Guinea) (ORIG/ARTN P520)))
  (ORIGIN/RELATION ((ORIG/ARTN P422) (ORIG/COLL Bevan1)))
  (ARTIFACTS/RELATION ((ARTF/TYPE container1) (ARTF/NUMB P422)))
  (ARTIFACTS/RELATION ((ARTF/NUMB P590) (ARTF/COND good1)))
  (ARTIFACTS/RELATION ((ARTF/NUMB P422) (ARTF/COND fragile1))))
```

TEXT A26

ARMSTRONG COLLECTED P56.
IT IS A BOX.
THIS CONTAINER IS SMALL.
HADDON COLLECTED P62 AND P63.
THESE ARTIFACTS ARE JUGS.

THE CONDITION OF THE JUGS IS POOR.
ARMSTRONG'S ARTIFACT COMES FROM MOUNT-HAGEN.
THE JUGS WERE COLLECTED IN WOODLARK.

```
((ORIGIN/RELATION ((ORIG/ARTN P56) (ORIG/COLL Armstrong1)))
 (ARTIFACTS/RELATION ((ARTF/TYPE container1) (ARTF/NUMB P56)))
 (ORIGIN/RELATION ((ORIG/COLL Haddon1) (ORIG/ARTN P63)))
 (ORIGIN/RELATION ((ORIG/COLL Haddon1) (ORIG/ARTN P62)))
 (ARTIFACTS/RELATION ((ARTF/TYPE container1) (ARTF/NUMB P63)))
 (ARTIFACTS/RELATION ((ARTF/TYPE container1) (ARTF/NUMB P62)))
 (ARTIFACTS/RELATION ((ARTF/COND poor2) (ARTF/NUMB P63)))
 (ARTIFACTS/RELATION ((ARTF/COND poor2) (ARTF/NUMB P62)))
 (ORIGIN/RELATION ((ORIG/ARTN P56) (ORIG/PLAC Mount-Hagen)))
 (ORIGIN/RELATION ((ORIG/PLAC Woodlark) (ORIG/ARTN P63)))
 (ORIGIN/RELATION ((ORIG/PLAC Woodlark) (ORIG/ARTN P62))))
```

TEXT A27

P4302 IS AN ARMLET.
P4370 IS A NECKLACE.
NILFISK COLLECTED THE ARMLET IN DAUI.
THE COLLECTOR WAS A NORWEGIAN ANTHROPOLOGIST.
HE COLLECTED THE NECKLACE IN WOODLARK.
HE COLLECTED P4360 WHICH IS AN ARMLET FROM THERE.
THE CONDITION OF THIS ONE IS GOOD.
THE CONDITION OF THE DAUI ARMLET IS POOR.

```
((ARTIFACTS/RELATION ((ARTF/TYPE ornament1) (ARTF/NUMB P4302)))
 (ARTIFACTS/RELATION ((ARTF/TYPE ornament1) (ARTF/NUMB P4370)))
 (ORIGIN/RELATION ((ORIG/COLL Nilfisk1) (ORIG/ARTN P4302) (ORIG/PLAC Daui)))
 (COLLECTORS/RELATION ((COLL/NAME Nilfisk1) (COLL/NATN Norwegian1)))
 (COLLECTORS/RELATION ((COLL/OCCP anthropologist1) (COLL/NAME Nilfisk1)))
 (ORIGIN/RELATION ((ORIG/COLL Nilfisk1) (ORIG/ARTN P4370) (ORIG/PLAC Woodlark)))
 (ARTIFACTS/RELATION ((ARTF/TYPE ornament1) (ARTF/NUMB P4360)))
 (ORIGIN/RELATION ((ORIG/COLL Nilfisk1) (ORIG/ARTN P4360) (ORIG/PLAC Woodlark)))
 (ARTIFACTS/RELATION ((ARTF/NUMB P4360) (ARTF/COND good1)))
 (ARTIFACTS/RELATION ((ARTF/NUMB P4302) (ARTF/COND poor2))))
```

TEXT A28

SMITH WHO WAS A BRITISH MISSIONARY COLLECTED P259.
P259 IS A NECKLACE WHICH COMES FROM DAUI.
P261 IS AN ARMLET.
THE CONDITION OF BOTH ARTIFACTS IS GOOD.
THE MISSIONARY COLLECTED P593 AND P594 FROM WOODLARK.
P593 IS A JUG.
P594 IS AN ARMLET.
THE CONDITION OF THIS ARTIFACT IS GOOD.
THE JUG IS POOR.

```
((COLLECTORS/RELATION ((COLL/NAME Smith1) (COLL/NATN British1)))
 (COLLECTORS/RELATION ((COLL/OCCP missionary1) (COLL/NAME Smith1)))
 (ORIGIN/RELATION ((ORIG/ARTN P259) (ORIG/COLL Smith1)))
 (ORIGIN/RELATION ((ORIG/ARTN P259) (ORIG/PLAC Daui)))
 (ARTIFACTS/RELATION ((ARTF/TYPE ornament1) (ARTF/NUMB P259)))
 (ARTIFACTS/RELATION ((ARTF/TYPE ornament1) (ARTF/NUMB P261)))
 (ARTIFACTS/RELATION ((ARTF/COND good1) (ARTF/NUMB P261)))
 (ARTIFACTS/RELATION ((ARTF/COND good1) (ARTF/NUMB P259)))
 (ORIGIN/RELATION ((ORIG/COLL Smith1) (ORIG/PLAC Woodlark) (ORIG/ARTN P594)))
 (ORIGIN/RELATION ((ORIG/COLL Smith1) (ORIG/PLAC Woodlark) (ORIG/ARTN P593)))
 (ARTIFACTS/RELATION ((ARTF/TYPE container1) (ARTF/NUMB P593)))
 (ARTIFACTS/RELATION ((ARTF/TYPE ornament1) (ARTF/NUMB P594)))
```

```
(ARTIFACTS/RELATION ((ARTF/COND good1) (ARTF/NUMB P594)))
(ARTIFACTS/RELATION ((ARTF/COND poor2) (ARTF/NUMB P593))))
```

TEXT A29

P957 AND P950 WERE COLLECTED BY SMITH.
THESE ARTIFACTS ARE JUGS.
THE COLLECTOR WAS A MISSIONARY.
P921 AND P922 WERE COLLECTED BY BEVAN.
THESE ARTIFACTS ARE SPEARS THAT CAME FROM DAUI.
BEVAN WAS A BRITISH ACADEMIC.
SMITH WAS AMERICAN.

```
((ORIGIN/RELATION ((ORIG/COLL Smith1) (ORIG/ARTN P950)))
 (ORIGIN/RELATION ((ORIG/COLL Smith1) (ORIG/ARTN P957)))
 (ARTIFACTS/RELATION ((ARTF/TYPE container1) (ARTF/NUMB P950)))
 (ARTIFACTS/RELATION ((ARTF/TYPE container1) (ARTF/NUMB P957)))
 (COLLECTORS/RELATION ((COLL/OCCP missionary1) (COLL/NAME Smith1)))
 (ORIGIN/RELATION ((ORIG/COLL Bevan1) (ORIG/ARTN P922)))
 (ORIGIN/RELATION ((ORIG/COLL Bevan1) (ORIG/ARTN P921)))
 (ORIGIN/RELATION ((ORIG/PLAC Daui) (ORIG/ARTN P922)))
 (ORIGIN/RELATION ((ORIG/PLAC Daui) (ORIG/ARTN P921)))
 (ARTIFACTS/RELATION ((ARTF/TYPE weapon1) (ARTF/NUMB P922)))
 (ARTIFACTS/RELATION ((ARTF/TYPE weapon1) (ARTF/NUMB P921)))
 (COLLECTORS/RELATION ((COLL/NAME Bevan1) (COLL/NATN British1)))
 (COLLECTORS/RELATION ((COLL/OCCP academic1) (COLL/NAME Bevan1)))
 (COLLECTORS/RELATION ((COLL/NAME Smith1) (COLL/NATN American1))))
```

TEXT A30

JONES WHO WAS A TRADER COLLECTED P350 FROM DAUI.
HE COLLECTED P370 FROM WOODLARK.
P350 IS A NECKLACE.
P370 IS AN ARMLET.
P391 IS A NECKLACE THAT COMES FROM WOODLARK.
THE CONDITION OF THESE ORNAMENTS IS GOOD.

ARMSTRONG AND HADDON WERE BRITISH.
THEY WERE ACADEMICS.
HADDON COLLECTED P597 AND P598 FROM DAUI.
THE ARTIFACTS ARE NECKLACES.
THE CONDITION OF THESE DAUI NECKLACES IS POOR.

P392 AND P393 ARE ARMLETS THAT WERE COLLECTED BY SMITH.
THIS COLLECTOR WAS A TRADER.
THE ARTIFACTS ARE FAIR.

```
((COLLECTORS/RELATION ((COLL/OCCP trader1) (COLL/NAME Jones)))
 (ORIGIN/RELATION ((ORIG/ARTN P350) (ORIG/COLL Jones) (ORIG/PLAC Daui)))
 (ORIGIN/RELATION ((ORIG/ARTN P370) (ORIG/COLL Jones) (ORIG/PLAC Woodlark)))
 (ARTIFACTS/RELATION ((ARTF/TYPE ornament1) (ARTF/NUMB P350)))
 (ARTIFACTS/RELATION ((ARTF/TYPE ornament1) (ARTF/NUMB P370)))
 (ORIGIN/RELATION ((ORIG/ARTN P391) (ORIG/PLAC Woodlark)))
 (ARTIFACTS/RELATION ((ARTF/TYPE ornament1) (ARTF/NUMB P391)))
 (ARTIFACTS/RELATION ((ARTF/COND good1) (ARTF/NUMB P391)))
 (ARTIFACTS/RELATION ((ARTF/COND good1) (ARTF/NUMB P350)))
 (ARTIFACTS/RELATION ((ARTF/COND good1) (ARTF/NUMB P370)))
 (COLLECTORS/RELATION ((COLL/NATN British1) (COLL/NAME Haddon1)))
 (COLLECTORS/RELATION ((COLL/NATN British1) (COLL/NAME Armstrong1)))
 (COLLECTORS/RELATION ((COLL/OCCP academic1) (COLL/NAME Haddon1)))
 (COLLECTORS/RELATION ((COLL/OCCP academic1) (COLL/NAME Armstrong1)))
 (ORIGIN/RELATION ((ORIG/PLAC Daui) (ORIG/ARTN P598) (ORIG/COLL Haddon1)))
 (ORIGIN/RELATION ((ORIG/PLAC Daui) (ORIG/ARTN P597) (ORIG/COLL Haddon1)))
```

(ARTIFACTS/RELATION ((ARTF/TYPE ornament1) (ARTF/NUMB P598)))
(ARTIFACTS/RELATION ((ARTF/TYPE ornament1) (ARTF/NUMB P597)))
(ARTIFACTS/RELATION ((ARTF/COND poor2) (ARTF/NUMB P598)))
(ARTIFACTS/RELATION ((ARTF/COND poor2) (ARTF/NUMB P597)))
(ORIGIN/RELATION ((ORIG/COLL Smith1) (ORIG/ARTN P393)))
(ORIGIN/RELATION ((ORIG/COLL Smith1) (ORIG/ARTN P392)))
(ARTIFACTS/RELATION ((ARTF/TYPE ornament1) (ARTF/NUMB P393)))
(ARTIFACTS/RELATION ((ARTF/TYPE ornament1) (ARTF/NUMB P392)))
(COLLECTORS/RELATION ((COLL/OCCP trader1) (COLL/NAME Smith1)))
(ARTIFACTS/RELATION ((ARTF/COND fair1) (ARTF/NUMB P393)))
(ARTIFACTS/RELATION ((ARTF/COND fair1) (ARTF/NUMB P392))))

TEXT A31

BEVAN COLLECTED P317 AND P325.
BOTH ARTIFACTS ARE CANOE-PROWS.
P219 IS A PADDLE THAT WAS COLLECTED BY ARMSTRONG.
ALL THREE ARTIFACTS COME FROM DAUI.
THE CONDITION OF BEVAN'S ARTIFACTS IS GOOD.

P719 IS A CANOE THAT WAS COLLECTED FROM WOODLARK.
IT WAS COLLECTED BY SMITH WHO WAS A TRADER.
THIS COLLECTOR WAS AMERICAN.
BEVAN WAS A BRITISH ACADEMIC.
P219'S COLLECTOR WAS A BRITISH MUSEUM-KEEPER.
HE COLLECTED P918 WHICH IS A CANOE-PROW.

((ORIGIN/RELATION ((ORIG/COLL Bevan1) (ORIG/ARTN P325)))
(ORIGIN/RELATION ((ORIG/COLL Bevan1) (ORIG/ARTN P317)))
(ARTIFACTS/RELATION ((ARTF/TYPE navigation/artifact) (ARTF/NUMB P317)))
(ARTIFACTS/RELATION ((ARTF/TYPE navigation/artifact) (ARTF/NUMB P325)))
(ORIGIN/RELATION ((ORIG/COLL Armstrong1) (ORIG/ARTN P219)))
(ARTIFACTS/RELATION ((ARTF/TYPE navigation/artifact) (ARTF/NUMB P219)))
(ORIGIN/RELATION ((ORIG/PLAC Daui) (ORIG/ARTN P317)))
(ORIGIN/RELATION ((ORIG/PLAC Daui) (ORIG/ARTN P325)))
(ORIGIN/RELATION ((ORIG/PLAC Daui) (ORIG/ARTN P219)))
(ARTIFACTS/RELATION ((ARTF/COND good1) (ARTF/NUMB P325)))
(ARTIFACTS/RELATION ((ARTF/COND good1) (ARTF/NUMB P317)))
(ORIGIN/RELATION ((ORIG/ARTN P719) (ORIG/PLAC Woodlark)))
(ARTIFACTS/RELATION ((ARTF/TYPE navigation/artifact) (ARTF/NUMB P719)))
(COLLECTORS/RELATION ((COLL/OCCP trader1) (COLL/NAME Smith1)))
(ORIGIN/RELATION ((ORIG/COLL Smith1) (ORIG/ARTN P719)))
(COLLECTORS/RELATION ((COLL/NAME Smith1) (COLL/NATN American1)))
(COLLECTORS/RELATION ((COLL/NAME Bevan1) (COLL/NATN British1)))
(COLLECTORS/RELATION ((COLL/OCCP academic1) (COLL/NAME Bevan1)))
(COLLECTORS/RELATION ((COLL/NAME Armstrong1) (COLL/NATN British1)))
(COLLECTORS/RELATION ((COLL/OCCP museum-keeper) (COLL/NAME Armstrong1)))
(ARTIFACTS/RELATION ((ARTF/TYPE navigation/artifact) (ARTF/NUMB P918)))
(ORIGIN/RELATION ((ORIG/COLL Armstrong1) (ORIG/ARTN P918))))

TEXT A32

THE CONDITION OF P971 IS GOOD.
HADDON COLLECTED IT.
HE WAS A BRITISH ACADEMIC.
BEVAN WAS A BRITISH MUSEUM-KEEPER.
HE COLLECTED P956.
THE CONDITION OF THIS ONE IS FAIR.
BOTH ARTIFACTS ARE SPEARS.

SMITH WHO WAS A GERMAN TRADER COLLECTED P316 WHICH IS AN ARROW.
HE COLLECTED P612 FROM WOODLARK.
THIS ARTIFACT IS A NECKLACE.

THE THREE WEAPONS COME FROM DAUI.
THE CONDITION OF THE ARROW IS GOOD.
THE ORNAMENT IS POOR.

```
((ARTIFACTS/RELATION ((ARTF/NUMB P971) (ARTF/COND good1)))
  (ORIGIN/RELATION ((ORIG/COLL Haddon1) (ORIG/ARTN P971)))
  (COLLECTORS/RELATION ((COLL/NAME Haddon1) (COLL/NATN British1)))
  (COLLECTORS/RELATION ((COLL/OCCP academic1) (COLL/NAME Haddon1)))
  (COLLECTORS/RELATION ((COLL/NAME Bevan1) (COLL/NATN British1)))
  (COLLECTORS/RELATION ((COLL/OCCP museum-keeper) (COLL/NAME Bevan1)))
  (ORIGIN/RELATION ((ORIG/ARTN P956) (ORIG/COLL Bevan1)))
  (ARTIFACTS/RELATION ((ARTF/NUMB P956) (ARTF/COND fair1)))
  (ARTIFACTS/RELATION ((ARTF/TYPE weapon1) (ARTF/NUMB P971)))
  (ARTIFACTS/RELATION ((ARTF/TYPE weapon1) (ARTF/NUMB P956)))
  (COLLECTORS/RELATION ((COLL/NAME Smith1) (COLL/NATN German1)))
  (COLLECTORS/RELATION ((COLL/OCCP trader1) (COLL/NAME Smith1)))
  (ARTIFACTS/RELATION ((ARTF/TYPE weapon1) (ARTF/NUMB P316)))
  (ORIGIN/RELATION ((ORIG/COLL Smith1) (ORIG/ARTN P316)))
  (ORIGIN/RELATION ((ORIG/ARTN P612) (ORIG/COLL Smith1) (ORIG/PLAC Woodlark)))
  (ARTIFACTS/RELATION ((ARTF/TYPE ornament1) (ARTF/NUMB P612)))
  (ORIGIN/RELATION ((ORIG/PLAC Daui) (ORIG/ARTN P316)))
  (ORIGIN/RELATION ((ORIG/PLAC Daui) (ORIG/ARTN P971)))
  (ORIGIN/RELATION ((ORIG/PLAC Daui) (ORIG/ARTN P956)))
  (ARTIFACTS/RELATION ((ARTF/NUMB P316) (ARTF/COND good1)))
  (ARTIFACTS/RELATION ((ARTF/NUMB P612) (ARTF/COND poor2))))
```

TEXT A33

P900 IS A SPEAR.
P700 IS AN ARMLET.
THIS ARTIFACT WAS COLLECTED IN DAUI.
IT IS COMMON.
THE WEAPON WAS COLLECTED FROM THERE.
P940 AND P950 ARE ARROWS.
P200 IS A SPEAR BLADE.

```
((ARTIFACTS/RELATION ((ARTF/TYPE weapon1) (ARTF/NUMB P900)))
  (ARTIFACTS/RELATION ((ARTF/TYPE ornament1) (ARTF/NUMB P700)))
  (ORIGIN/RELATION ((ORIG/ARTN P700) (ORIG/PLAC Daui)))
  (ORIGIN/RELATION ((ORIG/ARTN P900) (ORIG/PLAC Daui)))
  (ARTIFACTS/RELATION ((ARTF/TYPE weapon1) (ARTF/NUMB P950)))
  (ARTIFACTS/RELATION ((ARTF/TYPE weapon1) (ARTF/NUMB P940)))
  (ARTIFACTS/RELATION ((ARTF/TYPE weapon1) (ARTF/NUMB P200))))
```

Appendix B

Examples of the influence of context factor types

This appendix gives examples of the effects of particular types of context factor in instances of the application of context information to interpretation problems. As discussed elsewhere, the management of weights associated with context factors in the Capture system is not regarded as a precise theory about the relative importance of various factor types, but rather as an initial test of the context mechanism. The initial weights and degrading procedures used during the processing of all the examples in this appendix are those detailed in Section 6.2.

The numbers given are the differences in the contributions of major factor types to the activations of the best two candidates between which the choice was made when context was applied. Thus only contributions which were different are indicated, and negative numbers indicate contributions which were *against* the choice made by the system. The example texts were introduced in Section 6.5 and Section 6.7.

Example text A14

Plexir manufactures P9999 which is a computer.
It is supplied by Smith.
P1010 is a terminal that is supplied by Clark.
This one is made by Mikota.
These machines are red.

P9000 is a green printer.
It is made by Plexir.
P4444 is a blue computer.
The cost of the machine is 7850.
The peripheral is supplied by the P9999 supplier.
The terminal manufacturer makes the blue machine.
The cost of Mikota's peripheral is 235.

-- "This one is made by Mikota";
'make1' (manufacture) preferred to 'make8' (force).
Differences: association 136.

-- "P9000 is a green printer";
'printer2' (machine) preferred to 'printer1' (person).
Differences: subject-area 30; processing 8.

-- "It is made by Plexir";
'P9000' preferred to 'P1010' as referent for "It".
Differences: recency 116; emphasis 44; association -26; deixis -7; subject-area -7; processing 6.

Example text A18

Wintron manufactures P5050 which is a disc-drive.
P1010 is a computer which is made by this manufacturer.
It has a bolt.
P8770 is a printer that is made by Plexir.

Both peripherals are supplied by Clark.
Smith supplies the machine with the bolt.

P4740 is manufactured by P5050's manufacturer in London.
It is a micro-computer that is supplied by Jones.
He supplies P8800 which is a terminal.
The cost of the computer is 25.
The computers are red.
The three peripherals are green.

-- "He supplies P8800 which is a terminal";
'terminal1' (machine) preferred to 'terminal2' (place).
Differences: processing 16; association 12.

-- "The cost of the computer is 25";
'P4740' preferred to 'P1010' as referent for "the computer".
Differences: recency 78; emphasis 13; processing 2; association -2.

Example text A20

Plexir manufactures P9000.
It is a micro-computer.
Wintron manufactures P7000 which is a disc-drive.
P9000 is supplied by Smith.

P8000 is a computer.
It is supplied by Jones.
The status of this supplier is 10.
The status of P9000's supplier is 20.
The micro-computer is red.
The manufacturer manufactures P9090.

-- "The manufacturer manufactures P9090";
'Plexir1' preferred to 'Wintron1' as referent for manufacturer.
Differences: association 50.

<u>Example text A33</u>

P900 is a spear.
P700 is an armlet.
This artifact was collected in Daui.
It is common.
The weapon was collected from there.
P940 and P950 are arrows.
P200 is a spear blade.

-- "This artifact was collected in Daui";
'P700' preferred to 'P900' as referent for "This artifact".
Differences: recency 75; deixis 90; emphasis 34.

-- "It is common";
'P700' preferred to 'P900' as referent for "It".
Differences: recency 138; deixis 45; processing 32; emphasis 17.

-- "P940 and P950 are arrows";
'arrow1' (weapon) preferred to 'arrow2' (sign).
Differences: processing 10.

-- "P200 is a spear blade";
'blade1' (instrument) preferred to 'blade2' (man).
Differences: association 63; processing 3.

Example text from Section 6.5

P9999 is a disc-drive that is supplied by Smith.
This peripheral is manufactured by Mikota.
He supplies P7777 which is a terminal.
It is manufactured in London by Plexir.
Clark supplies P9000 which is manufactured by Marconi in Paris.

-- "Clark supplies P9000 which is manufactured by Marconi in Paris";
'manufacture/loc' preferred to 'supplies/loc' as a derived structure relationship.
Differences: association 56; processing 12.

Example text from Section 6.5

P500 is an armlet.
It was collected by Haddon.
P550 is red.

P9000 is a disc-drive that is supplied by Smith.
The cost of the machine is 200.
P9900 is red.

-- "P550 is red";
'relp/artifact/colour' preferred to 'relp/machine/colour' as underlying database predicate.
Differences: processing 6.

-- "P9900 is red";
'relp/machine/colour' preferred to 'relp/artifact/colour' as underlying database predicate.
Differences: task 20; processing 8.

References

Birnbaum, L. 1985. Lexical Ambiguity as a Touchstone for Theories of Language Analysis. *Proceedings of IJCAI-85*, Los Angeles: 815-820.

Bobrow, D. and T. Winograd. 1977. An Overview of KRL, a Knowledge Representation Language. *Cognitive Science* 1: 3-46.

Bobrow, R. J. and B.L. Webber. 1980. Knowledge Representation for Syntactic/Semantic Processing. *Proceedings of AAAI-1*, Pittsburgh: 316-323.

Boguraev, B. K. 1979. Automatic Resolution of Linguistic Ambiguities (PhD thesis). Technical Report No. 11, Computer Laboratory, Cambridge University.

Boguraev, B. K. and K. Sparck Jones. 1982. A Natural Language Analyser for Database Access. *Information Technology: Research and Development* 1: 23-39.

Boguraev, B. K. and K. Sparck Jones. 1983. How to Drive a Database Front End Using General Semantic Information. *Proceedings of the ACL Conference on Applied Natural Language Processing*, Santa Monica: 81-88.

Borkin, S. A. 1980. *Data Models: A Semantic Approach for Database Systems.* Cambridge, Mass.: MIT Press.

Brachman, R. J. 1978. A Structural Paradigm for Representing Knowledge (PhD thesis). Technical Report No. 3605, Bolt Beranek and Newman Inc., Cambridge, Mass.

Brachman, R. J. 1979a. Taxonomy, Descriptions, and Individuals in Natural Language Understanding. *Proceedings of the 17th Annual Meeting of the ACL*, San Diego: 33-37.

Brachman, R. J. 1979b. On the Epistemological Status of Semantic Networks. In: N.V. Findler (ed.), *Associative Networks*. New York: Academic Press.

Brachman, R. J., V. P. Gilbert, and H. J. Levesque. 1985. An Essential Hybrid Reasoning System: Knowledge and Symbol Level Accounts of KRYPTON. *Proceedings of IJCAI-85*, Los Angeles: 532-539.

Bundy, A. 1979. What's The Difference? Predicate Calculus and Semantic Nets (Again). *AISB Quarterly*, October 1979: 8-9.

Cater, A. W. S. 1981. Analysis and Inference for English (PhD thesis). Technical Report No. 19, Computer Laboratory, Cambridge University.

Chamberlin, D. D., M. M. Astrahan, K. P. Eswaran, P. P. Griffiths, R. A. Lorie, J. W. Mehl, P. Reisner, and B. W. Wade. 1976. SEQUEL 2: A Unified Approach to Data Definition, Manipulation, and Control. *IBM Journal of Research and Development* 20: 560-575.

Charniak, E. 1978. On the Use of Framed Knowledge in Language Comprehension. *Artificial Intelligence* 11: 225-265.

Charniak, E. 1981. The Case-Slot Identity Theory. *Cognitive Science* 5: 285-289.

Charniak, E. 1982. Context Recognition in Language Comprehension. In: W. G. Lehnert and M. H. Ringle (eds), *Strategies for Natural Language Processing*. Hillsdale, New Jersey: Lawrence Erlbaum Associates.

Charniak, E. 1983. Passing Markers: A Theory of Contextual Influence in Language Comprehension. *Cognitive Science* 7: 171-190.

Correira, A. 1980. Computing Story Trees. *American Journal of Computational Linguistics* 6: 135-149.

Cowie, J. R. 1983. Automatic Analysis of Descriptive Texts. *Proceedings of the ACL Conference on Applied Natural Language Processing*, Santa Monica: 117-123.

Date, C. J. 1981. *An Introduction to Database Systems*, 3rd Edition. Reading, Mass.: Addison-Wesley.

DeJong, G. 1979. Prediction and Substantiation: A New Approach to Natural Language Processing. *Cognitive Science* 3: 251-273.

Deliyani, A. and P. A. Kowalski. 1979. Logic and Semantic Networks. *Communications of the ACM* 22: 184-192.

Fahlman, S. E. 1979. *NETL: A System for Representing and Using Real-World Knowledge*. Cambridge, Mass.: MIT Press.

Fahlman, S. E. 1980. Preliminary Design for a Million-Element NETL Machine. *Proceedings of AAAI-1*, Pittsburgh: 249-252.

Fahlman, S. E., D. S. Touretzky and W. van Roggen. 1981. Cancellation in a Parallel Semantic Network. *Proceedings of IJCAI-81*, Vancouver: 257-264.

Gazdar, G., E. Klein, G. K. Pullum and I. A. Sag. 1985. *Generalized Phrase Structure Grammar*. Oxford: Blackwell.

Gray, M. A. 1981. Implementing Unknown and Imprecise Values in Databases. In: S.M. Deen and P. Hammersley (eds), *Databases (Proceedings of the First British National Conference on Databases)*, London: Pentech Press.

Grosz, B. J. 1977. The Representation and Use of Focus in Dialogue Understanding (PhD thesis). SRI Technical Note No. 151, SRI International, Menlo Park, California.

Grosz, B. J. (ed.). 1981. Research on Natural Language Processing at SRI. SRI Technical Note No. 257, SRI International, Menlo Park, California.

Grosz, B. J., N. Haas, G. Hendrix, J. Hobbs, P. Martin, R. Moore, J. Robinson, and S. Rosenschein. 1982. DIALOGIC: A Core Natural-language Processing System. *Proceedings of the Ninth International Conference on Computational Linguistics*, Prague: 95-100.

Grosz, B. J., A. K. Joshi, and S. Weinstein. 1983. Providing a Unified Account of Definite Noun Phrases in Discourse. *Proceedings of the 21st Annual Meeting of the ACL*, Cambridge, Mass.: 44-50.

Grosz, B. J. and C. L. Sidner. 1985. Discourse Structure and the Proper Treatment of Interruptions. *Proceedings of IJCAI-85*, Los Angeles: 832-839.

Hayes, Patrick J. 1977a. In Defence of Logic. *Proceedings of IJCAI 5*, Cambridge, Mass.: 559-565.

Hayes, Philip J. 1977b. On Semantic Nets, Frames and Associations. *Proceedings of IJCAI 5*, Cambridge, Mass.: 99-107.

Hendrix, G. G. 1978. Encoding Knowledge in Partitioned Networks. SRI Technical Note No. 164, SRI International, Menlo Park, California.

Hillis, W. D. 1981. The Connection Machine. AI Memo 646, Artificial Intelligence Laboratory, MIT.

Hirst, G. 1983. A Foundation for Semantic Interpretation. Technical Report CS-83-03, Department of Computer Science, Brown University.

Hirst, G. and E. Charniak. 1982. Word Sense and Case Slot Disambiguation. *Proceedings of AAAI-82*, Pittsburgh: 95-98.

Hobbs, J. R. 1981. Metaphor Interpretation as Selective Inferencing. *Proceedings of IJCAI-81*, Vancouver: 85-91.

Kamp, H. 1981. A Theory of Truth and Semantic Representation. In: J. A. G. Groenendijk, T. M. V. Janssen, and M. B. J. Stokhof (eds), *Formal Methods in the Study of Language*, Part I, Amsterdam: Mathematisch Centrum.

Kantor, R. N. 1977. The Management and Comprehension of Discourse Connection by Pronouns in English (PhD thesis). Department of Linguistics, Ohio State University.

Kaplan, M. K. and J. Bresnan. 1982. Lexical-Functional Grammar: A Formal system for Grammatical Representation. In: J. Bresnan (ed.), *The Mental Representation of Grammatical Relations*, Cambridge, Mass.: MIT Press.

Kaplan, S. J. and J. Davidson. 1981. Interpreting Natural Language Database Updates. *Proceedings of the 19th Annual Meeting of the ACL*, Stanford: 139-141.

Katz, J. J. and J. A. Fodor. 1963. The Structure of a Semantic Theory. *Language* 39: 170-210.

Kay, M. 1980. The Proper Place of Men and Machines in Language Translation. Report No. CSL-80-11, Xerox Palo Alto Research Center, California.

King, T. J. 1979. The Design of a Relational Database Management System for Historical Records (PhD thesis). University of Cambridge.

Lebowitz, M. 1981. The Nature of Generalization in Understanding. *Proceedings of IJCAI-81*, Vancouver: 348-353.

Lebowitz, M. 1983. Intelligent Information Systems. *Proceedings of the 6th ACM SIGIR Conference*, Bethesda: 25-29.

Lehnert, W. G., M. G. Dyer, P. N. Johnson, C. J. Yang, and S. Harley. 1983. BORIS - An Experiment in In-Depth Understanding of Narratives. *Artificial Intelligence* 20: 15-62.

Maier, D. and S. C. Salveter. 1982. Supporting Natural Language Updates in Database Systems. *Proceedings of the European Conference on Artificial Intelligence*, Orsay: 244-249.

Marcus, M. P. 1980. *A Theory of Syntactic Recognition for Natural Language*. Cambridge, Mass.: MIT Press.

Mark, W. 1981. Representation and Inference in the Consul System. *Proceedings of IJCAI-81*, Vancouver: 375-381.

Martin, W. A. 1980. Roles, Co-Descriptors, and the Formal Representation of Quantified English Expressions. Technical Manual 139, Laboratory for Computer Science, MIT.

McDermott, D. V. 1975. Very Large Planner Type Data Bases. AI Memo 339, Artificial Intelligence Laboratory, MIT.

McDonald, D. B. 1982. Understanding Noun Compounds (PhD thesis). Report CMU-CS-82-102, Department of Computer Science, Carnegie-Mellon University.

McDonald, D. D. 1981. Language Production: the Source of the Dictionary. *Proceedings of the 19th Annual Meeting of the ACL*, Stanford: 57-62.

Mellish, C. S. 1980. Some Problems in Early Noun Phrase Interpretation. *Proceedings of the AISB Conference*, Amsterdam.

Minsky, M. L. 1975. A Framework for Representing Knowledge. In: P. H. Winston (ed.), *The Psychology of Computer Vision*, New York: McGraw-Hill.

Moore, R. C. 1986. The Role of Logic in Intelligent Systems. In: I. Benson (ed.), *Intelligent Machinery*, Cambridge: Cambridge University Press.

Norton, L. M. 1983. Automated Analysis of Instructional Text. *Artificial Intelligence* 20: 307-344.

Procter, P. (ed.). 1978. *Longman Dictionary of Contemporary English*. Harlow and London: Longman.

Quillian, M. R. 1968. Semantic Memory. In: M. Minsky (ed.), *Semantic Information Processing*, Cambridge, Mass.: MIT Press.

Reimer, U. and U. Hahn. 1983. A Formal Approach to the Semantics of a Frame Data Model. *Proceedings of IJCAI-83*, Karlsruhe: 337-339.

Reinhart, T. 1983. *Anaphora and Semantic Interpretation*. London: Croom Helm.

Rieger, C. J. 1975. Conceptual Memory and Inference. In: R. C. Schank, N. M. Goldman, C. J. Rieger, and C. K. Riesbeck (eds), *Conceptual Information Processing*, Amsterdam: North-Holland.

Ritchie, G. D. 1976. Problems in Local Semantic Processing. *Proceedings of the AISB Conference*, Edinburgh: 234-241.

Ritchie, G. D. 1977. Computer Modelling of English Grammar. Thesis CST-1-77, Department of Computer Science, University of Edinburgh.

Ritchie, G. D. and F. K. Hanna. 1983. Semantic Networks - A General Definition and A Survey. *Information Technology: Research and Development* 2: 187-231.

Sager, N. 1981. *Natural Language Information Processing*. Reading, Mass.: Addison-Wesley.

Schank, R. C. 1975. SAM - A Story Understander. Research Report No. 43, Yale AI Project, Department of Computer Science, Yale University, New Haven.

Schank, R. C. 1982a. Reminding and Memory Organization: An Introduction to MOPs. In: W. G. Lehnert and M. H. Ringle (eds), *Strategies for Natural Language Processing*, Hillsdale, New Jersey: Lawrence Erlbaum Associates.

Schank, R. C. 1982b. *Dynamic Memory*. Cambridge: Cambridge University Press.

Schmolze, J. G. and T. A. Lipkis. 1983. Classification in the KL-ONE Knowledge Representation System. *Proceedings of IJCAI-83*, Karlsruhe: 330-332.

Schubert, L. K., R. G. Goebel, and N. J. Cercone. 1979. The Structure and Organization of a Semantic Net for Comprehension and Inference. In: N.V. Findler (ed.), *Associative Networks*, New York: Academic Press.

Shapiro, S. C. 1979. The SNePS Semantic Network Processing System. In: N. V. Findler (ed.), *Associative Networks*, New York: Academic Press.

Sidner, C. L. 1979. Towards a Computational Theory of Definite Anaphora Comprehension in English Discourse (PhD thesis). Technical Report AI-TR-537, Artificial Intelligence Laboratory, MIT, Cambridge, Mass.

Small, S. 1980. Word Expert Parsing: A Theory of Distributed Word-based Natural Language Understanding (PhD thesis). Technical Report No. 954, Department of Computer Science, University of Maryland.

Sparck Jones, K. 1983a. Compound Noun Interpretation Problems. In: *Computer Speech Processing*, SERC/CREST-ITG Advanced Course Lecture Notes, Cambridge, England.

Sparck Jones, K. 1983b. Shifting Meaning Representations. *Proceedings of IJCAI-83*, Karlsruhe: 621-623.

Steinacker, I. and H. Trost. 1983. Structural Relations - A Case Against Case. *Proceedings of IJCAI-83*, Karlsruhe: 627-629.

Tait, J. I. 1982. Automatic Summarising of English Texts (PhD thesis). Technical Report No. 47, Computer Laboratory, University of Cambridge.

Tait, J. I. and K. Sparck Jones. 1983. Automatic Search Term Variant Generation for Document Retrieval. R&D Report No. 5793, British Library.

Vilain, M. 1985. The Restricted Language Architecture of a Hybrid Representation System. *Proceedings of IJCAI-85*, Los Angeles: 547-551.

Walker, D. E. 1978. *Understanding Spoken Language.* New York: Elsevier North-Holland.

Waltz, D. L. 1978. An English Language Question Answering System for a Large Relational Database. *Communications of the ACM* 21: 526-539.

Waltz, D. L. 1981. Toward a Detailed Model of Processing for Language Describing the Physical World. *Proceedings of IJCAI-81*, Vancouver: 1-6.

Wilensky, R. 1981. A Knowledge-based Approach to Language Processing: A Progress Report. *Proceedings of IJCAI-81*, Vancouver: 25-30.

Wilensky, R. 1982. Talking to Unix In English: An Overview of an On-line UNIX Consultant. Report No. UCB/CSD82/104, Department of Computer Science, University of California, Berkeley.

Wilks, Y. 1973. An Artificial Intelligence Approach to Machine Translation. In: R. C. Schank and K. M. Colby (eds), *Computer Models of Thought and Language*, San Francisco: W.H. Freeman and Company.

Wilks, Y. 1975a. An Intelligent Analyser and Understander of English. *Communications of the ACM*, 18: 264-274.

Wilks, Y. 1975b. A Preferential, Pattern-matching Semantics for Natural Language Understanding. *Artificial Intelligence* 6: 53-74.

Wilks, Y. 1977. Good and Bad Arguments about Semantic Primitives. *Communication and Cognition* 10: 181-221.

Wilks, Y. 1978. Making Preferences More Active. *Artificial Intelligence* 11: 197-223.

Winograd, T. 1972. *Understanding Natural Language.* Edinburgh: Edinburgh University Press.

Woods, W. A. 1970. Transition Network Grammars for Natural Language Analysis. *Communications of the ACM* 13: 591-606.

Woods, W. A. 1973. An Experimental Parsing System for Transition Network Grammars. In: R. Rustin (ed.), *Natural Language Processing*, New York: Algorithmics Press.

Woods, W. A. 1978a. Research in Natural Language Understanding. Report No. 3797, Bolt Beranek and Newman Inc., Cambridge, Mass.

Woods, W. A. 1978b. Semantics and Quantification in Natural Language Question Answering. *Advances in Computers* 17: 1-87.

Zdybel, F., N. R. Greenfeld, M. D. Yonke, and J. Gibbons. 1981. An Information Presentation System. *Proceedings of IJCAI-81*, Vancouver: 978-984.

Index

For EU product safety concerns, contact us at Calle de José Abascal, 56–1°,
28003 Madrid, Spain or eugpsr@cambridge.org.

www.ingramcontent.com/pod-product-compliance
Ingram Content Group UK Ltd.
Pitfield, Milton Keynes, MK11 3LW, UK
UKHW010046140625
459647UK00012BB/1649

* 9 7 8 0 5 2 1 1 0 3 5 8 9 *